OXFORD
UNIVERSITY PRESS

ASPIRE
SUCCEED
PROGRESS

Complete Chemistry for Cambridge Secondary 1

Philippa
Gardom Hulme

TEACHER PACK

Oxford excellence for Cambridge Secondary 1

OXFORD

OXFORD
UNIVERSITY PRESS

Great Clarendon Street, Oxford OX2 6DP

Oxford University Press is a department of the University of Oxford.
It furthers the University's objective of excellence in research,
scholarship, and education by publishing worldwide in

Oxford   New York

Auckland   Cape Town   Dar es Salaam   Hong Kong   Karachi
Kuala Lumpur   Madrid   Melbourne   Mexico City   Nairobi
New Delhi   Shanghai   Taipei   Toronto

With offices in

Argentina   Austria   Brazil   Chile   Czech Republic   France   Greece
Guatemala   Hungary   Italy   Japan   Poland   Portugal   Singapore
South Korea   Switzerland   Thailand   Turkey   Ukraine   Vietnam

© Oxford University Press 2013

The moral rights of the author have been asserted

Database right Oxford University Press (maker)

First published 2013

British Library Cataloguing in Publication Data

Data available

ISBN: 978-0-19-839020-6
10

Printed in Great Britain by Ashford Colour Press Ltd, Gosport, Hampshire

Acknowledgements

® IGCSE is the registered trademark of Cambridge International Examinations.

The publisher would like to thank Cambridge International Examinations for
their kind permission to reproduce past paper questions.

Cambridge International Examinations bears no responsibility for the
example answers to questions taken from its past question papers which are
contained in this publication.

Cover photo: Olivier Le Queinec / Shutterstock

Welcome to your **Complete Chemistry for Cambridge Secondary 1** Teacher Pack. This Teacher Pack has been written to provide classroom support and teaching materials across all three stages of Cambridge Secondary 1.

Your Teacher Pack includes a book of lesson plans as well as answers to all of the Student Book and Workbook questions for your reference at any time. The accompanying CD-ROM includes a wide variety of additional resources to support you and your students in the classroom.

Using your book

This book contains suggested lesson plans and answers to all of the questions in the Student Book and Workbook.

There is one lesson plan for every spread in the Student Book, including enquiry and extension pages. Each lesson plan suggests activities for use in the classroom linked to the topics covered on the Student Book spread.

Each lesson plan begins with a reference to the pages of the Student Book that it covers and a summary of their objectives. Any key words from the Student Book pages are included at the bottom of the page.

The *Overview* section of the lesson plan reviews what the suggested activities will cover to fulfil the learning objectives. Here you will also find advice and tips about common misconceptions, what you may need to review from the Cambridge Primary curriculum framework or previous lessons, and suggested questions for a class discussion.

The *Activities* section of the lesson plan lists several different activities that can be used in the classroom. These activities include fun and engaging demonstrations, interesting practical ideas, group work suggestions, reading and research activities, and ways to explore a novel topic using models, class discussions or Internet research.

Lesson plans that are matched to enquiry spreads include activities that encourage students to use the skills they are learning about by planning and carrying out their own investigations, analysing data, and drawing conclusions individually or as part of a group.

Most of the lessons have suggested *Extension* activities to stretch your strongest students and help prepare them for the step up to Cambridge IGCSE®. Some of these could be carried out in class, whilst others could be set as homework.

Every spread in the Student Book is matched to a page in the Workbook. At the end of each lesson plan the corresponding workbook page is suggested as *Homework*.

There are lots of extra resources on the CD to accompany every lesson plan. These are listed in the *CD Resources* box at the top of the page, and suggestions on how they can be used are given in the *Activities* section of the lesson plan.

At the back of this book are the answers for all of the questions in both the Student Book and Workbook for quick reference in the classroom.

Using your CD-ROM

The CD-ROM that accompanies this book contains additional resources to support you in the classroom.

Every lesson plan in the book is also found on the CD-ROM as both a PDF, for easy printing, and as a Word document, so that you can tailor the lesson to your classroom and your students' needs.

All of the extra worksheets listed on the lesson plans can be found on the CD-ROM as Word documents, so that they can be added to or changed as required. Most of these worksheets are a single page so that they are easy to print and photocopy.

Extra worksheets for each chapter focus on the scientific vocabulary introduced in that chapter. These will help support lower ability students or students that speak English as an additional language.

There are animations that can be used on an interactive whiteboard or screen at the front of the class. They cover topics that are difficult to explain using words and pictures in the Student Book, these include particles in changes of state, dissolving, and particles in metals.

Some of the diagrams from the Student Book have been reproduced as slideshows that you can use at the front of the class. These diagrams have been reproduced with and without labels, so that they can be used to elicit answers from students or even to start a discussion.

Table of contents

CD resources

- Worksheet 1.1.1
- Worksheet 1.1.2
- Worksheet 1.1.3

Objective

- Use ideas about particles to explain the behaviour of substances in the solid, liquid, and gas states

Overview

This lesson introduces the simple particle model, which explains changes of state, and properties such as expansion. A more complex particle model, involving atoms and bonding, explains chemical change. Students meet this model later in the course.

A common misconception is that solids, liquids, and gases are different types of matter. To avoid students picking up this idea, this course emphasises that any one substance can exist in three states. The particles do not change, only their arrangement and behaviour.

Activities

- Students imagine they had a bar of chocolate. Could they cut it into smaller and smaller pieces for ever? Greek philosophers asked a question like this 2500 years ago. Two of them – Leucippus and Democritus – thought that matter is divided into tiny separate bits, with empty space between. This is the particle theory of matter. It is a scientific model that explains observations. There is more about Leucippus and Democritus on page 95 of the Student book.

- Display diagrams of the particle arrangements of a substance in its three states. Describe the behaviour of the particles in each state.

- Students examine samples of substances and decide whether each is in its solid, liquid, or gas state. How might the particle model explain observed properties? **Worksheet 1.1.1** supports this activity.

- **Practical activity (first part):** Demonstrate trying to compress samples of sand, water, and air in sealed syringes. Students use the particle model to explain their observations. Part 1 of **worksheet 1.1.2** supports this activity.

- **Practical activity (second part):** Demonstrate trying to open the metal lid on a tightly closed jar. Pour hot water over the lid – it is easier to open. Explain that the metal has expanded. This is because the particles vibrated more, so taking up more space. The particles themselves have not expanded. Part 2 of **worksheet 1.1.2** supports this activity.

Extension

Worksheet 1.1.3 summarises learning from the whole lesson.

Homework

Workbook page 7

Key words

particles, states, solid, liquid, gas, compress, expands, contracts

Student book, pages 10–11

CD resources

- Worksheet 1.2.1
- 1.2 Changes of state illustration

Objectives

- Name the changes of state involving liquids and gases
- Explain changes of state using ideas about particles

Overview

The lesson starts with a look at wax and at water in different states, and a reminder about how particles behave in these states. Students then consider changes of state involving liquids and gases. They measure the boiling point of water, and display their results in the form of a line graph. To finish the lesson, students use ideas about particles to explain boiling, evaporating, and condensing. They act out these changes of state.

The illustration from page 10 of the Student book is included on the CD-ROM with and without labels. This could be used as plenary activity to find out what students already know about changes of state.

Activities

- Burn a candle. Elicit that the wax exists in three states – solid, liquid, and gas. It is the gas that burns. Boil some water. Elicit that the water is present in two states – as a liquid, and as a gas (steam). This lesson focuses on changes of state involving liquids and gases.

- **Practical activity:** Students do an experiment to find the temperature at which liquid water boils. They display their results as line graphs. **Worksheet 1.2.1** supports this activity.

- Students read the section on *Liquid to gas* on page 10 of the Student book. Student pairs discuss differences between boiling and evaporation, and use ideas about particles to explain these differences.

- Students read the section on *Gas to liquid* on page 11 of the Student book. They draw diagrams to show what happens to the particles during condensation.

Extension

As a class, act out boiling, evaporation, and condensation. Each student takes the role of one particle.

Homework

Workbook page 8

Key words

ice, steam, evaporation, boiling, boiling point, condensation

CD resources
- Worksheet 1.3.1
- Worksheet 1.3.2
- Scientific investigation flowchart

Objective

- Understand why questions, evidence, and explanations are important in science

Overview

This lesson takes students through one process by which scientists develop explanations, and which is summarised in the flow chart on page 13 of the Student book. Students start by discussing a selection of questions – which could be answered scientifically? This leads to the point that scientific questions are ones that the collection of evidence will help to answer. The lesson then focuses on one question – why does water boil at different temperatures in different places? Students use evidence to test a possible explanation for this question.

The flowchart on page 13 of the Student book is included on the CD-ROM with and without the text. This flowchart can be used to guide students through the process of developing scientific theories.

Activities

- Student pairs discuss the questions on **worksheet 1.3.1**. Which could be answered scientifically? Make the point that scientific questions are ones that the collection of evidence will help to answer.

- Student book pages 12–13 (for teacher reference – do not show students at this stage). Tell students that water boils at different temperatures in Mumbai, a city by the sea, and Leh, a city in the mountains (use local examples if possible). Ask students to suggest a scientific question based on this evidence, for example: *Why does water boil at different temperatures in different places?* Begin building up a flow chart with this question at the top (Student book page 13).

- Suggest an explanation to the question in the previous activity – boiling point depends on altitude. Add this stage to the flow chart (Student book page 13).

- **Worksheet 1.3.2** (first part): Ask students how they could test the explanation suggested in the previous activity. Students plot line graphs of boiling temperature vs. altitude. Add this stage to the flow chart (Student book page 13).

- **Worksheet 1.3.2** (second part): Students check the evidence supports the explanation. Add this stage to the flow chart. Point out that scientific explanations may lead to more questions!

Homework

Workbook page 9

Key words

question, evidence, explanation

CD resource
- Worksheet 1.4.1

Objectives

- Name and explain changes of state involving solids
- Describe how melting points help identify substances

Overview

This lesson explains changes of state involving solids. It starts by getting students to think about particles – how does their behaviour change when a solid melts, or a liquid freezes? Students then plot heating and cooling curves for stearic acid, to find its melting point. There is then a short demonstration in which students learn that melting temperatures give information about both the purity and identity of a substance. The lesson ends with a demonstration to illustrate the process of sublimation.

Activities

- Lead a discussion to elicit how particle behaviour changes on melting and freezing. As a class, students act out melting and freezing, with each student taking the role of one particle.

- Students follow the guidance to plot heating and cooling curves for stearic acid, to find its melting point. **Worksheet 1.4.1** supports this activity.

- Explain that melting temperatures indicate the purity of a substance – if a substance has a sharp melting point, it is pure. If a material melts over a range of temperatures, it is not pure. Illustrate this point by inserting a thermometer into solid butter or ghee (mixtures) and heating gently to melt. Students melted a pure substance in the previous activity. Melting point data also help identify substances – students read about this on page 14 of the Student book.

- Use solid iodine to demonstrate sublimation. Place one iodine crystal in a sealed container. Warm it gently with your hands. A purple vapour forms. Students take on the roles of particles to act out sublimation.

Homework

Workbook page 10

Key words

melting, melting point, pure substance, freezing, freezing point, sublimation, sublime

CD resources
- Worksheet 1.5.1
- Particles animation

Objective
- Use ideas about energy to explain changes of state

Overview

In this lesson, students use ideas about energy to explain changes of state. The main activity is a group activity, in which students work together to answer four key questions: How can we use ideas about energy to explain boiling, evaporation, melting, and freezing? Student groups then create posters or short plays to demonstrate what they have learnt.

The **particles animation** on the CD-ROM shows what happens to particles in solids, liquids, and gases when the temperature increases or decreases.

Activities

- Student pairs speculate about why substances change state – what makes a solid melt, or a gas condense?

- Divide students into groups of four. These are *home groups*. Within home groups, each student is allocated one question from **worksheet 1.5.1**.

  Students doing the same question then get together in new groups of three or four. These are *expert groups*. Expert groups tackle the questions using information from the Student book, and plan how to teach their home groups what they have learnt.

  Students return to their home groups, and teach each other what they have learnt.

- Students remain in home groups. They create posters or short plays to demonstrate what they have learnt about energy and state changes.

- Home groups present their posters or plays to one other group. The other group peer assesses. Part 5 of the **worksheet 1.5.1** supports this activity.

Homework
Workbook page 11

Key words
energy, boiling, evaporation, particles, melting, freezing

CD resources

- Worksheet 1.6.1
- Worksheet 1.6.2
- Worksheet 1.6.3
- Dissolving animation

Objectives

- Use particle theory to explain dissolving
- Understand what a secondary source is
- Practise making conclusions from data

Overview

The lesson begins by a demonstration of dissolving salt in water, and a matching activity to reinforce the meanings of key words. Students then observe a second demonstration to show that total mass is conserved when a substance dissolves in a solvent. The next activity involves students using rice and dried beans to model the particles when a solute dissolves in a solvent. Finally, students learn about saturated solutions and solubility. They draw bar charts using data from a secondary source, and make conclusions from the data. **Worksheets 1.6.2** and **1.6.3** review work that students would have done as part of the Primary curriculum framework.

The **dissolving animation** on the CD-ROM shows what happens to solute particles when they are dissolved in a solvent.

Activities

- Demonstrate dissolving one spatula measure of salt in water. Use the words solvent, solute, solution, dissolve, and soluble. Student pairs use cards to match these words – and others – to their definitions. **Worksheet 1.6.1** supports this activity.
- Demonstrate that mass is conserved when a substance dissolves by pouring water into a beaker and measuring the mass. Add a known mass of salt and stir to dissolve. Show that:

  mass of solution = mass of solute + solvent

  Students record the results on Part A of **worksheet 1.6.2**.
- Students follow the guidance on Part B of **worksheet 1.6.2** to model dissolving using rice and dried beans.
- Demonstrate adding sugar (sucrose) to 100 cm³ of water, one spoonful at a time. Students guess how many spoonfuls will dissolve. At 25 °C, 200 g of sugar dissolves in 100 cm³ of water. This is approximately 40 teaspoonfuls. Explain what a saturated solution is. Part C of **worksheet 1.6.2** supports this activity.
- Students follow the guidance to draw bar charts on solubility, using data from a secondary source. They make conclusions from the data. **Worksheet 1.6.3** supports this activity.

Homework

Workbook page 12

Key words

dissolve, solution, solvent, solute, saturated solution, solubility, soluble, secondary source, scientific journal

CD resources
- Worksheet 1.7.1
- Worksheet 1.7.2

Objective

- Understand the processes involved in planning an investigation

Overview

The purpose of this lesson is to teach students to plan investigative work, and for students to obtain evidence about the relationship between temperature and solubility for one solute. The lesson starts with a reminder about solubility from lesson 1.6 – how much sugar dissolves in water? Students then speculate about the effect of temperature on the solubility of sugar, before planning their investigations. They will go through the following stages – suggesting ideas to test, considering variables, outlining a plan, making predictions, choosing apparatus, making observations and measurements, and presenting evidence in tables. The investigation continues in lesson 1.8.

Activities

- Demonstrate dissolving sugar in water, to remind students of the fourth activity of lesson 1.6. Student pairs speculate about the effect of temperature on sugar solubility.

- Student pairs discuss ideas they could test to investigate the effect of temperature on solubility, and suggest questions to investigate. Discuss some of these as a class. Pairs finalise their investigation questions.

- Students plan an investigation on the effect of temperature on the solubility of a particular substance. Guidance is given on **worksheet 1.7.1**, but students are likely to need further help. It would be useful to display the apparatus. Suitable solutes include sodium hydrogencarbonate, potassium chloride, or ammonium chloride. **Worksheet 1.7.2** also supports this activity.

- Students carry out their investigations and collect their results in a table. **Worksheet 1.7.2** supports this activity.

Extension

Students use the Internet to research solubility curves.

Homework

Workbook page 13

Key words

prediction, variables, fair test, measuring cylinder, beaker, thermometers, balance, electric balance, Bunsen burner, stirring rod

CD resources
- Worksheet 1.8.1
- Worksheet 1.8.2

Objective

- Present evidence in tables and line graphs

Overview

In this lesson, students continue the investigation they started in lesson 1.7. They decide whether to present their evidence in a line graph or bar chart, and then produce line graphs. Students then write a conclusion for the investigation, and discuss what to do about any results that do not fit into the pattern. The lesson finishes with a matching activity to remind students of key terms from lessons 1.6 to 1.8 – some of the cards are repeated from lesson 1.6.

Activities

- Discuss the evidence obtained in lesson 1.7. Is it easy to make conclusions from the evidence presented in tables? Elicit that it would be better to present the evidence graphically.

- Student pairs discuss whether to draw bar charts or line graphs. Tell students that bar charts are suitable if the variable you change is discrete. Line graphs are suitable if the variable you change is continuous. In this investigation, line graphs should be drawn.

- Students draw line graphs and write conclusions for their investigations. **Worksheet 1.8.1** supports this activity.

- As a class, discuss any results which do not fit into a pattern. Discuss what could be done about these.

- Student pairs match key words to definitions to remind themselves of key terms from lessons 1.6 – 1.8. **Worksheet 1.8.2** supports this activity.

Homework

Workbook page 14

Key words

discrete, continuous, range, line graph

CD resources
- Worksheet 2.1.1
- Worksheet 2.1.2

Objectives
- Understand what materials are
- Explain what an element is
- Find metals and non-metals on the periodic table
- Give examples of elements

Overview
The lesson begins with a look at materials – how many can students see? What are their properties? Students are then introduced to elements as substances from which all materials are made, and which cannot be split up. They examine the properties of as many elements as possible, and find them in the periodic table. Finally, there is an optional research activity in which each student finds out key facts about one element.

Activities
- Students list the materials they can see, and describe their properties. Make sure they give properties of the materials, not of the objects made from them.
- Explain that every material is made from one or more elements. Elements cannot be split up. There are 92 elements found naturally on Earth. Every element is made of its own type of particle, which is unique to that element. If possible, play the element song – search the Internet for *element song*. The *privatehand* animation is recommended. Part A of **worksheet 2.1.1** supports this activity.
- Tell students that the periodic table lists all the elements. Elements on the left of the stepped line are metals. Elements on the right are non-metals. Students should look at page 27 of the Student book.
- Students examine real samples of as many elements as possible, note their properties, and find them in the periodic table. Make the point that every element has unique properties. Part B of **worksheet 2.1.1** supports this activity.

Extension
Each student uses the Internet to research a different element. They produce small posters for display. **Worksheet 2.1.2** supports this activity.

Homework
Workbook page 15

Key words
materials, properties, periodic table, metals, non-metals

CD resources

- Worksheet 2.2.1
- Worksheet 2.2.2
- Worksheet 2.2.3

Objectives

- Identify typical metal properties
- Link the properties of two metals to their uses

Overview

The lesson starts with an opportunity to elicit student's prior knowledge of metals and their properties. There is also a short matching activity to ensure that students understand the meanings of words describing properties. Students then do a practical activity to explore the properties of metals (and non-metals) in more detail. The lesson ends with a card sorting activity to reinforce the properties of typical metals.

Activities

- Students look at Part B of **worksheet 2.1.1** from lesson 2.1. They use the properties they recorded to pick out metal elements from those they examined. The purpose of this activity is to elicit students' prior knowledge about metals and their properties.
- Student pairs match cards to build knowledge of vocabulary that describes properties. **Worksheet 2.2.1** supports this activity.
- Students test the following properties for a selection of elements: thermal and electrical conduction, hardness, and appearance. They pick out the properties that are typical of metals. **Worksheet 2.2.2** supports this activity.
- Students sort cards to reinforce their knowledge of typical metal properties. **Worksheet 2.2.3** supports this activity.

Extension

Students use the Student book to find out how the properties of gold and iron are linked to their uses, or the Internet to discover how the properties of other metals determine their uses.

Homework

Workbook page 16

Key words

sonorous, strong, hard, density, malleable, ductile

CD resources
- Worksheet 2.3.1
- Worksheet 2.3.2

Objectives

- Identify typical non-metal properties
- Link the properties of non-metals to their uses

Overview

This lesson develops learning from the previous lesson by providing opportunities for students to explore the properties of typical non-metal elements. First, students pick out typical non-metal properties from the property cards they used at the end of lesson 2.2. They then examine samples of non-metal elements to check that they have these properties. Students next present melting point and boiling point data on bar charts. Finally, students explore links between the uses and properties of some non-metal elements.

Activities

- Students return to the card sort activity from the end of lesson 2.2. This time, they pick out properties that are typical of non-metal elements and record these. **Worksheet 2.2.3** completed in the previous lesson supports this activity. Look at page 30 of the Student book.

- Students examine a selection of non-metal elements and check – as far as is possible – that they have the properties identified in the previous activity.

- Students plot bar charts of melting point and boiling point data, and answer the questions on **worksheet 2.3.1** based on their charts. Lead a discussion to elicit that, in general, metals have higher melting and boiling points than non-metals. Point out some exceptions – mercury has a relatively low melting point (it is liquid at room temperature) and carbon has high melting and boiling points.

- Students use the Student book to explore the links between the uses and properties of some non-metal elements. They record their findings as a table or poster. **Worksheet 2.3.2** supports this activity.

Extension

Students use the Internet to discover how the properties of other non-metal elements determine their uses.

Homework

Workbook page 17

Key words

brittle, semiconductor, semi-metal, metalloid

Student book, pages 32–33

♂ CD resources
- Worksheet 2.4.1
- Worksheet 2.4.2

Objective

- Practise drawing conclusions from data in tables and graphs

Overview

This lesson focuses on making conclusions from data in tables and graphs, and also examines what to do when results do not fit an expected pattern. Students begin by doing an experiment to compare the time taken for heat to move along different metal rods. They write a conclusion for their investigation. There is a then a short demonstration on stretching springs. What can an experimenter do if one result does not fit the expected pattern?

Activities

- Show students strips or rods of four metals. Pairs discuss how they could find out which of the metals is the best conductor of heat.
- Students follow the guidance on the sheets to finish planning, and to carry out, an experiment to compare the time taken for heat to move along different metal rods. They use their data to draw a conclusion for the investigation. **Worksheets 2.4.1** and **2.4.2** support this activity.
- Demonstrate the investigation shown on the lower half of page 33 in the Student book, in which masses are added to a spring and the extension of the spring is measured. Show students the graph in the Student book, in which one result does not fit the pattern. Student pairs discuss what the experimenter could do about this result. Tell students that the experimenter could repeat the extension reading at this force twice more – if both results now fit the pattern they could ignore the first result.
- If time permits, students answer the questions in the Student book.

Homework

Workbook page 18

Key words

anomalous, metal, non-metal, conductor, bar chart, line graph, conclusion

CD resource
- Worksheet 2.5.1

Objectives

- Know what alloys are
- Give examples of alloys and their properties and uses
- Explain why alloys have different properties from the elements in them

Overview

This lesson is about alloys. It begins with an opportunity for students to share what they already know about alloys. It continues with a group activity, in which students work together to answer four key questions: What are alloys, and how are their properties different from those of their elements? Why are the properties of alloys different from those of their elements? What is steel, and why and how is it useful? What is bronze, and why and how is it useful?

Activities

- Student pairs discuss what they already know about alloys, including common alloys such as steel. Ask a few pairs to feed back.
- Divide students into groups of four. These are *home groups*. Within home groups, each student is allocated one question from **worksheet 2.5.1**.

  Students doing the same question then get together in new groups of three or four. These are *expert groups*. Expert groups tackle the questions using information from the Student book, and plan how to teach their home groups what they have learnt.

  Students return to their home groups, and teach each other what they have learnt.
- Students remain in home groups. Ask them a few questions – perhaps to tackle as a group test – so as to check learning from the previous activity.

Extension

Students research shape memory alloys, such as nitinol. Typing *shape memory alloy* into a search engine yields useful websites.

Homework

Workbook page 19

Key words

alloy, steel, bronze, particle arrangement, properties

CD resource
- Worksheet 2.6.1

Objective

- Describe everyday materials and their physical properties

Overview

The lesson draws on knowledge and understanding about properties from lesson 2.2. It begins with a look at everyday materials around the room. What properties does a material have? Why do these properties make the material suitable for its uses? Students then do a practical activity in which they examine various materials and record their properties. They discuss which of a material's properties make it suitable for a particular use of the material. The lesson finishes with a poster-making activity.

Activities

- Student pairs discuss the materials they can see around the room. What properties does a material have? Why do these properties make the material suitable for its uses? Make sure that students discuss properties of materials, not objects that are made from them.

- Student groups follow the guidance on **worksheet 2.6.1** to carry out a practical activity. This involves recording the properties of a material, and choosing one way in which the material is used. Students then choose the properties that make the material suitable for this use. Lead a class discussion to draw out key points from this activity.

- Students make posters using pages 36–7 of the Student book as a starting point. Give them a choice of two themes:

  - A poster about the uses of several materials, and why their properties make them suitable for these uses.

  - A poster advertising one material, its uses, and why its properties make it suitable for these uses.

Homework

Workbook page 20

Key words

brittle, flexible, stiff, strong, hard, soft, conductor, absorbent, waterproof

CD resources
- Worksheet 2.7.1
- Worksheet 2.7.2

Objective

- Understand what polymers are and how they are used

Overview

This lesson starts with an introduction to polymers, both natural and synthetic – what are they? How do their physical properties make them suitable for their uses? Students then investigate the physical properties of five polymers, and consider how their properties make them suitable for their uses. The next activity involves answering questions based on data about polymer properties. The lesson ends with an explanation of the properties of poly(ethene).

Activities

- Display a selection of objects made from polymers, both natural and synthetic. Student pairs discuss how the properties of the polymers make them suitable for these uses. Tell students that polymers are made up of very long particles.

- Students examine objects made from different polymers and note their properties. They answer questions based on their findings. Suitable polymers for this activity can be found by looking at the recycling symbols on plastic objects. **Worksheet 2.7.1** supports this activity.

- Students study data about five polymers, and answer questions based on the data. **Worksheet 2.7.2** supports this activity.

- Teacher explains why poly(ethene) is strong and flexible, based on the explanation on page 38 of the Student book.

Homework

Workbook page 21

Key words

polymer, synthetic polymer, natural polymer

CD resources

- Worksheet 3.1.1
- Worksheet 3.1.2

Objectives

- Give examples of acids and alkalis
- Compare the properties of acids and alkalis
- Make conclusions from data

Overview

This lesson introduces acids and alkalis. Students begin by considering whether acids are harmful or useful. They then look at examples of acids and alkalis, and record their properties. At this stage, alkalis are simply regarded as the chemical opposites of acids. Finally, students analyse data on sulfuric acid production.

Activities

- Students choose where to stand on an imaginary line with *acids are dangerous* written at one end and *acids are useful* at the other end. Ask some students to justify their positions on the line.
- Student groups sort cards into two piles – examples of acids being useful, and examples of acids being harmful. This activity is designed to generate discussion. **Worksheet 3.1.1** supports this activity.
- Students list all the acids they have heard about so far, and, where possible, note down their properties and uses. They use the Student book to make similar notes about alkalis. Part 1 of **worksheet 3.1.2** supports this activity.
- Students place cards on the table to show typical properties of acids and alkalis. Part 2 of **worksheet 3.1.2** supports this activity.
- Students answer question 4 on page 43 of the Student book to make conclusions from data presented in a pie chart.

Homework

Workbook page 22

Key words

acid, corrosive, alkalis

CD resources

- Worksheet 3.2.1
- Worksheet 3.2.2
- Worksheet 3.2.3

Objectives

- Know the pH of acidic, alkaline, and neutral solutions
- Use indicators to measure pH
- Choose suitable apparatus

Overview

This lesson builds on lesson 3.1. It begins by encouraging students to see the need for distinguishing acids from alkalis – and hence the need for indicators. Students then make their own indicator from red cabbage or hibiscus flowers. Finally, students learn about the pH scale.

Activities

- Display a bottle containing a colourless solution. Students discuss how to find out whether the solution is acidic, alkaline, or neither. Could they drink it? Put it on their skin?

  Display a second, identical, bottle with a *corrosive* hazard label. Does this help them decide? Point out that none of the suggestions are good ideas – the first two are risky, and both acidic and alkaline solutions can be corrosive.

- Introduce the idea of indicators by dropping dilute hydrochloric acid, dilute sodium hydroxide, and pure water onto red and blue litmus paper.

- Students follow the instructions on **worksheet 3.2.1** to make a natural indicator. They calibrate the indicator by observing its colours in known acidic, alkaline, and neutral solutions. Finally, they use their indicator to test an unknown solution.

- Students answer the questions on **worksheet 3.2.2** to reinforce their learning so far.

- Demonstrate the colours of Universal Indicator in solutions of different pH. Students tackle the questions on **worksheet 3.2.3**. Read page 44 of the Student book.

Homework

Workbook page 23

Key words

litmus indicator, Universal Indicator, dilute, concentrated

Student book, pages 46–47

CD resources
- Worksheet 3.3.1
- Worksheet 3.3.2

Objectives

- Understand what neutralisation is
- Give examples of applications of neutralisation

Overview

This lesson begins with a brief demonstration – rainbow in a burette – to remind students that the pH scale is continuous. Students then carry out a practical to illustrate the process of neutralisation and the pH changes that occur during the process. There is then an optional extension activity, in which students work out how to reverse the neutralisation process they have just carried out. The lesson concludes with an opportunity to apply ideas about neutralisation to soil pH and crop choices.

Activities

- Demonstrate that the pH scale is continuous by making a 'rainbow' in a burette:
  - Mix 20 cm^3 0.1 mol/dm^3 sodium hydroxide with Universal Indicator to get a strong colour. Pour into a burette.
  - Add 10 cm^3 sodium hydrogencarbonate solution (2 spatula measures dissolved in 10 cm^3 pure water).
  - Add 10 cm^3 0.1 mol/dm^3 hydrochloric acid.
  - Place a bung over the end of the burette. Hold it with your thumb and invert to mix. Allow to settle.
  - Observe the rainbow, and question students about the pH in different regions. Why is it neutral in the middle?
- Students do a practical to illustrate neutralisation and the pH changes that occur during the process. **Worksheet 3.3.1** supports this activity.
- Students apply ideas about neutralisation to soil pH and crop choices. **Worksheet 3.3.2** supports this activity.

Extension

Students consider how to reverse the neutralisation process on **worksheet 3.3.1**, and test their ideas.

Homework

Workbook page 24

Key words

neutralise, neutralisation, acid rain

CD resources

- Worksheet 3.4.1
- Worksheet 3.4.2

Objective

- Understand how to plan an investigation, and collect and consider evidence

Overview

In this lesson, students plan and carry out an investigation to compare different types of indigestion tablet. The lesson begins by discussing how to choose ideas to test, and how to decide which variables to control, change, and observe. Students then plan their investigations and, having checked with the teacher, carry them out. Students then use their collected data to make conclusions.

Activities

- Display a variety of indigestion tablets, and tell students that they work by neutralising excess stomach acid. Student pairs discuss ideas to test to compare the tablets, and suggest questions they could investigate. Create a class list of suitable questions, for example: *Which type of tablet causes the greatest increase in pH when added to acid?*

- Ask pairs to list possible variables. Discuss these as a class – if investigating the question above, which should they control, change, and observe?

- Students follow the guidance on **worksheet 3.4.1** to help them plan their investigations. Having confirmed their plans are suitable, they carry out their investigations. **Worksheet 3.4.2** also supports this activity.

- Students make conclusions from their collected data. Discuss these as a class. **Worksheet 3.4.2** supports this activity.

Homework

Workbook page 25

Key words

pH, neutralise, suggesting ideas, variable, anomalous

Student book, pages 52–53

CD resources
- Worksheet 4.1.1
- 4.1 Structure of the Earth illustration

Objectives
- Describe a model for the structure of the Earth
- Explain how we know about the Earth's structure

Overview

The lesson begins with a brief look at evidence for the Earth being spherical. It continues with an activity in which students create posters or models to represent the structure of the Earth and the states of each of its layers. The lesson finishes with an optional activity about a recent proposal to drill into the mantle. What will we learn from this research? Why should it be funded?

The illustration from page 52 of the Student book is included on the CD-ROM with and without labels. This could be used as plenary activity to find out what students already know about the structure of the Earth.

Activities
- Students pairs role play a discussion that might have taken place many years ago about the shape of the Earth. One student uses evidence from their own observations to assert that the Earth is flat. The other student uses evidence described on page 52 of the Student book to support their view that the Earth is spherical.
- Display an egg that has been boiled for about 10 minutes in its shell. Cut it in half. Tell students that the egg is a model for the structure of the Earth. Pairs use pages 52–3 of the Student book to discuss similarities and differences between the modern model of the structure of the Earth, and the egg model.
- Students make posters or models to represent the modern model of the structure of Earth. They add detailed labels to their models, giving the state of each layer. Models could be made from plasticine or clay. Use pages 52–3 of the Student book.

Extension

Students use the information on **worksheet 4.1.1** to write a request for funding for a research project to drill to the Earth's mantle.

Use the Internet to research how ideas about the shape of the Earth changed over time. The Wikipedia article *Flat Earth* is a suitable starting point.

Homework

Workbook page 26

Key words

scientific model, crust, mantle, outer core, inner core

Student book, pages 54–55

CD resource

■ Worksheet 4.2.1

Objectives

- Describe the properties of igneous rocks
- Give examples of igneous rocks
- Explain how igneous rocks were formed
- Link igneous rock properties to their uses

Overview

The lesson begins by looking at a sample of granite, and speculating how it was formed. Students then examine the crystallisation of liquid salol in warm and cool conditions to help explain why different samples of igneous rocks have different-sized crystals. The lesson continues with an opportunity to study the properties of igneous rocks, and an optional research activity.

Activities

- Give student groups samples of granite, or any other igneous rock. Ask students to speculate how they were formed.

- Students now study a model to illustrate how granite was formed. Begin with a quick demonstration – place a few drops of liquid salol on a microscope slide. Observe as the liquid cools and solidifies. Tell students that some rocks, such as granite, formed when liquid rock cooled and solidified to form crystals. These are igneous rocks. The liquid rock may have cooled underground, on the surface, or under the sea.

- Students follow the guidance on **worksheet 4.2.1** to do an investigation to compare rocks formed when magma cools underground and under the sea. Smaller crystals form quickly on the cooler slide.

- Students observe samples of different igneous rocks with a hand lens. What do they have in common? They are all made up of interlocking crystals.

Extension

Use the Student book and the Internet to research how the properties of different igneous rocks determine their uses.

Homework

Workbook page 27

Key words

granite, igneous rock, magma, crystals, basalt, non-porous, minerals

CD resources
- Worksheet 4.3.1
- Worksheet 4.3.2

Objectives
- Describe sedimentary rock properties
- Identify and name sedimentary rocks

Overview
This lesson begins with an introduction to some differences between igneous and sedimentary rocks. Students then do tests to distinguish sedimentary rocks from rocks of other types. The lesson continues with the production of a poster about the properties of particular sedimentary rocks, and how their properties are linked to their uses. Finally, students consider what they know about the formation of sedimentary rocks, in preparation for lesson 4.4.

Activities
- Student groups each examine one igneous rock, for example granite, and one sedimentary rock, for example limestone or sandstone. Elicit the differences.
- Students follow the guidance on **worksheet 4.3.1** to do tests to distinguish sedimentary rocks from rocks of other types.
- Students use the Student book and the Internet to research the properties and uses of different sedimentary rocks, for example sandstone, claystone, mudstone, and limestone. They display their findings on posters. **Worksheet 4.3.2** supports this activity.
- Finish the lesson with a short discussion in pairs. What do students know about how sedimentary rocks are formed? The next lesson will build upon this knowledge.

Homework
Workbook page 28

Key words
sedimentary rock, porous, grains

CD resources
- Worksheet 4.4.1
- Worksheet 4.4.2
- Worksheet 4.4.3
- Worksheet 4.4.4

Objectives
- Explain how rocks are weathered
- Explain how sediments form rocks

Overview

In this lesson, through a series of experiments, students model the different stages by which sedimentary rocks are formed. They use an acidic solution and calcium carbonate powder to simulate the chemical weathering of limestone. They shake rocks in bottles to simulate physical weathering. Students use sand and water to model deposition and transport, and coins and matchsticks to help them picture compaction and cementation.

Activities
- Begin by referring back to the final activity of lesson 4.3 – what do students know about sedimentary rock formation? Refer to the flow diagram on Student book page 57. The purpose of this lesson is to explain each stage shown.
- Students follow the guidance to do the five activities on **worksheets 4.4.1–4**. These could be set up around the room, allowing students to move from one activity to another. Activities can be tackled in any order. Students record their findings.
- Return to the flow diagram on page 57, and ask students to describe and explain what the models taught them about each stage.

Extension

Students consider the models in the second activity – how are they like, and unlike, the actual processes?

Homework

Workbook page 29

Key words

weathering, sediments, chemical weathering, physical weathering, biological weathering, transportation, erosion, deposition, compaction, cementation

CD resources
- Worksheet 4.5.1
- Worksheet 4.5.2
- Worksheet 4.5.3

Objectives

- Explain how metamorphic rocks are made
- Identify metamorphic rocks
- Give examples of metamorphic rocks

Overview

The lesson begins with a practical activity in which students compare the properties of limestone and marble. Students then complete a writing frame to explain how metamorphic rocks are formed, and how to recognise them. They then make model fossils, and subject them to various forces, as can happen when a sedimentary rock is subjected to pressure as it becomes a metamorphic rock.

Activities

- Tell students that marble and limestone are different types of rock, but that both types of rock consist mainly of the same compound, calcium carbonate. Students follow the guidance on **worksheet 4.5.1** to compare the properties of the two rocks. Make the point that the rocks look and feel different, but the change observed on adding acid is the same for both rock types.

- Students use the Student book to help them complete the writing frame on **worksheet 4.5.2** to explain how metamorphic rocks are made, and to describe how to recognise them. As an extension activity, students could use the Internet to add detail to their notes.

- Students make model fossils, and – during the process – squash them in one of three possible directions. Once the models are dry, they exchange with another group who must work out the direction in which the fossils were squashed. The formation of fossils is covered in detail in lesson 4.9. **Worksheet 4.5.3** supports this activity.

Homework

Workbook page 30

Key words

metamorphic rock, slate, gneiss, marble

Student book, pages 62–63

CD resources

- Worksheet 4.6.1
- Worksheet 4.6.2

Objectives

- To understand why questions, evidence, and explanations are important in science
- To interpret the rock cycle

Overview

Students start by reading about the observations and explanations of two early scientists – Ibn Sina and Chu Hsi. Next, they look carefully at the rock cycle in the Student book and observe as the teacher uses wax to demonstrate one possible route around the rock cycle. The lesson finishes with a rock cycle communication challenge – can students explain the rock cycle to a particular audience?

Activities

- Students read about the observations and explanations of two early scientists – Ibn Sina and Chu Hsi on pages 62–3 of the Student book. They speculate as to why early scientists were interested in the Earth and the formation of its features.
- Teacher uses the diagram in the Student book to help explain the rock cycle. Teacher then uses the wax model described on **worksheet 4.6.1** to demonstrate one possible route around the rock cycle.
- Student groups follow the guidance on **worksheet 4.6.2** to plan how to communicate the rock cycle to a particular audience. Groups then share their plans with another group, and peer assess.

Extension

Ask students to suggest rock cycle processes not represented by the wax model. The final row of the table on **worksheet 4.6.1** supports this activity.

Homework

Workbook page 31

Key words

geologist, rock cycle, uplift

Student book, pages 64–65

⊙ CD resources

- Worksheet 4.7.1
- Worksheet 4.7.2
- Worksheet 4.7.3
- 4.7 Volcanic eruption illustration

Objective

- Understand how scientists use science to explain predictions

Overview

The lesson begins with an introduction to the work of vulcanologists, and a sequencing activity based on this. Next, there is a demonstration of a tiltmeter – how does it work? Why are data from tiltmeters useful? The third activity is a short role play in which students take the roles of vulcanologists explaining to government officials the scientific explanations for their predictions. A final activity is an opportunity for students to consider the work of vulcanologists. During the lesson, it is vital to make the point that scientists can never be sure exactly when a volcano will erupt.

The illustration from page 64 of the Student book is included on the CD-ROM with and without labels. This could be used as plenary activity to find out what students already know about volcanoes.

Activities

- Teacher tells students that vulcanologists make observations and measurements, look for patterns in their data, and use these patterns to help them make predictions about future volcanic activity. Students sequence the tasks on Part A of **worksheet 4.7.1**.
- Teacher demonstrates the action of a tiltmeter using the guidance on **worksheet 4.7.2**.
- Student pairs role play a vulcanologist explaining to a government official the scientific explanations for their predictions. Part B of **worksheet 4.7.1** supports this activity.
- Students plan and present talks on the work of vulcanologists for a school careers day. **Worksheet 4.7.3** supports this activity.

Extension

Use the Internet to research recent or local volcanic eruptions. Find out what the volcano emitted, and the impacts of the eruption.

Homework

Workbook page 32

Key words

magma, lava, volcano, vulcanologist

Student book, pages 66–67

CD resources
- Worksheet 4.8.1
- Worksheet 4.8.2
- Worksheet 4.8.3

Objectives
- List soil components
- Name soil types
- Describe soil properties

Overview
This lesson introduces soil types and properties. It is linked to lesson 4.9, in which students study soil in further detail. The lesson starts by setting up a practical to look at the components of a soil sample. Lesson 4.9 provides an opportunity to classify the soil based on the relative amounts of different sized rock fragments. Students then compare the texture and drainage of three different soil samples, and use their findings to attempt to classify the samples. Finally, students make notes about the origins and roles of soil components.

Activities
- Students set up the apparatus on Part A of **worksheet 4.8.1**, to separate soil components. They return to this in lesson 4.9.
- Students compare the texture and drainage properties of three different soil samples. Later, they will attempt to classify each soil. **Worksheet 4.8.2** supports this activity.
- Teacher describes the components of soil and the origin and role of each component. Students complete the written tasks on **worksheet 4.8.3** using the Student book to help them.
- Students examine their results from the second activity. They record their observations and answer the questions on **worksheet 4.8.2**.

Homework
Workbook page 33

Key words
rock fragments, humus, clay soil, loam, sandy soil

CD resources

- Worksheet 4.8.1 (from lesson 4.8)
- Worksheet 4.9.1
- Worksheet 4.9.2

Objectives

- Describe soil properties
- Explain why soil properties are important

Overview

This lesson continues the work on soil started in lesson 4.8. Students begin by returning to the first activity of lesson 4.8, and try classifying the soil based on the relative amounts of different sized rock fragments. Students then do a practical to measure the volume of air in a soil sample. Finally, students test soil pH for several samples, and suggest crops that might grow well in the samples.

Activities

- Students return to their apparatus set up from lesson 4.8, and follow the guidance on part B of **worksheet 4.8.1** to try classifying the soil based on the relative amounts of different sized rock fragments. Students will not be able to make firm classifications based on their findings; rather, the results give some indication of whether the soil is sandy, clay, or loam.
- Students measure the air content of a soil sample. **Worksheet 4.9.1** guides them through this activity.
- Students measure the pH of different soil samples and suggest crops that might grow well in each sample. **Worksheet 4.9.2** supports this activity.

Homework

Workbook page 34

Key words

pore, secondary source, minerals

Student book, pages 70–71

CD resources

- Worksheet 4.10.1
- 4.10 Stages of fossilisation illustrations

Objectives

- State what a fossil is
- Describe how fossils form
- Give examples showing what we can learn from the fossil record

Overview

This lesson is about fossils. It begins with an opportunity for students to share what they already know about fossils. It continues with a group activity, in which students work together to answer three key questions: What are fossils, and why do they form only rarely? How do fossils form? What have we learnt from fossils? There is then an optional activity in which students research recent fossil finds.

The six illustration from page 70 of the Student book is included on the CD-ROM in sequence. This could be used to show students how fossilisation occurs.

Activities

- Student pairs discuss what they already know about fossils. What are fossils? What type of rock are they found in? What have we learnt from fossils? Ask a few pairs to feed back.

- Divide students into groups of three. These are *home groups*. Within home groups, each student is allocated one question from **worksheet 4.10.1**.

  Students doing the same question then get together in new groups of three or four. These are *expert groups*. Expert groups tackle the questions using information from the Student book, and plan how to teach their home groups what they have learnt.

  Students return to their home groups, and teach each other what they have learnt.

- Students remain in home groups. Ask them a few questions – perhaps to tackle as a group test – so as to check learning from the previous activity.

Extension

Students research recent fossil finds. Typing *fossils* into the news section of a search engine yields interesting articles.

Homework

Workbook page 35

Key words

fossil, preserved, remains, palaeontologist, fossil record

CD resource
- Worksheet 4.11.1

Objective

- Describe how scientists have estimated the age of the Earth

Overview

The lesson begins with a short role play about William Thomson's ideas about the age of the Earth. Students are then introduced to sedimentary rock strata and their relative ages. Next, they learn about index fossils, and apply their new knowledge to create the strata in a cliff face – complete with fossils – and to compare their cliff face with that of another student. The lesson ends by telling students the modern best estimate of the age of the Earth.

Activities

- Ask students how old the Earth is. Note down their answers to refer to at the end of the lesson.

- Students read about William Thomson's ideas about the age of the Earth on page 72 of the Student book. In pairs, they perform quick role plays of a conversation between Thomson and a modern scientist – how do we now know that Thomson's estimate for the age of the Earth is incorrect?

- Explain that sedimentary rocks are laid down in layers called *strata*. Lower strata are older – they were formed first. Describe the work of William Smith, who recognised that rock strata of the same age contain the same fossils, and that certain fossils are only found in rock strata of certain ages.

- Student pairs create a poster of strata in a cliff face, complete with index fossils. They compare their posters to those of other students. **Worksheet 4.11.1** supports this activity.

- Tell students that the oldest rocks on Earth are 4 600 000 000 000 years old. This is the best estimate for the age of the Earth. How does this value compare to student estimates in the first activity?

Homework

Workbook page 36

Key words

strata, index fossil, radiometric dating

Student book, pages 74–75

CD resources
- Worksheet 4.12.1
- Worksheet 4.12.2

Objective

- Describe what fossils tell us about our human past

Overview

The lesson begins with an account of the find of the fossilised remains of a young girl in Ethiopia. Students then match evidence from the find to possible explanations. The lesson continues with an Internet research activity, in which students find out more about one of three fossil finds described in the student book – Toumaï, the Laetoli footprints, or *Homo floresiensis*. Finally, students share their findings with others.

Activities

- Show a video clip about the discovery of the fossilised remains of a young girl in Ethiopia – Selam. Alternatively, ask students to read about the fossil find on page 74 of the Student book.
  Excellent video clips can be found for searching for:
  Zeresenay Alemseged TED
  Zeresenay Alemseged National Geographic
  Zeresenay Alemseged Nature video
  It is recommended that you watch the video clips before the lesson to check their suitability for your students.

- Students match evidence from the fossilised remains of Selam to suitable explanations. **Worksheet 4.12.1** supports this activity.

  Students read about three further fossil finds on pages 74–5 of the Student book – Toumaï, the Laetoli footprints, and *Homo floresiensis*. They choose one of these finds to research on the Internet in greater detail, and include information about how evidence from the find supports explanations about the find. Some suitable web links are included on **worksheet 4.12.2**.

Homework

Workbook page 37

Key words

human, fossil, radiometric dating, ancestor, descendent

Student book, pages 80–81

⊙ **CD resources**
■ Worksheet 5.1.1
■ Camping gas animation

Objectives

● Describe and explain the properties of substances in their solid, liquid, and gas states
● Identify changes of state

Overview

This lesson revises and reinforces the content of lessons 1.1, 1.2, and 1.4. Its primary purpose is to use the particle model to explain differences in the properties of a substance in their three states. Students will also revisit particle explanations of changes of state. The main task in this lesson is a group activity, in which students work together to answer four key questions. Student groups then create posters to demonstrate what they have learnt.

The **camping gas animation** on the CD-ROM shows the properties of a gas. The particles are compressed close together in the canister and then spread out to fill the space when they are released.

Activities

● Display samples of water in its solid, liquid, and gas states (as ice, liquid water, and steam). Briefly elicit some differences between the properties of water in its different states.

● Divide students into groups of four. These are *home groups*. Within home groups, each student is allocated one question from **worksheet 5.1.1.**

Students doing the same question then get together in new groups of three or four. These are *expert groups*. Expert groups tackle the questions using information from the Student book, and plan how to teach their home groups what they have learnt.

Students return to their home groups, and teach each other what they have learnt.

● Students remain in home groups. They create posters to demonstrate what they have learnt (or reminded themselves) about the states of matter and changes of state.

● Home groups show their posters to one other group. The other group peer assesses. Part 5 of **worksheet 5.1.1** supports this activity.

Homework

Workbook page 38

Key words

solid, liquid, gas, particle arrangement, particle theory, condensation, freezing, melting, evaporation, boiling

CD resources
- Worksheet 5.2.1
- Worksheet 5.2.2

Objectives
- Use the particle theory to explain diffusion
- Describe evidence for diffusion

Overview

This lesson introduces the idea of diffusion as the random movement and mixing of particles. The lesson begins with a short demonstration in which students use their sense of smell to detect diffusion. Students then investigate the effect of temperature on the speed of diffusion of potassium manganate(VII) in water. Finally, there is a demonstration to show the diffusion of ammonia and hydrogen chloride. By the end of the lesson students should know that diffusion happens faster at higher temperatures, and that big, heavy particles diffuse more slowly than smaller, lighter particles.

Activities
- Place an item with a strong smell, for example air freshener, at the front. Students raise their hands when they detect the smell. A few students act out what they think happens to the particles. Discuss the role play as a class. Tell students that diffusion – the random movement and mixing of particles – has occurred.
- Quickly demonstrate the diffusion of potassium manganate(VII) in water. Students then plan and carry out an investigation to find out about the effect of water temperature on the speed of diffusion. **Worksheets 5.2.1** and **5.2.2** support this activity.

  Demonstrate the diffusion of ammonia and hydrogen chloride along a long tube, as on Student book page 82. Explain that ammonium chloride forms at the hydrogen chloride end because hydrogen chloride particles are bigger and heavier than ammonia particles, so diffuse more slowly. For detailed instructions, see *www.nuffieldfoundation.org/practical-chemistry* and search for *diffusion*.

Homework
Workbook page 39

Key words
diffusion, temperature, particle size, particle mass

Student book, pages 84–85

CD resources
- Worksheet 5.3.1
- Worksheet 5.3.2

Objectives
- Use a formula to calculate density
- Explain why different substances have different densities

Overview

The lesson begins with a practical introduction to density – which of two identically-sized bags has the greater mass? Students then measure the mass and volume of various objects and calculate the density of the materials they are made from. The lesson finishes with a group task, in which student pairs find out about how the closeness of particles, and particle mass, can be used to explain density. Groups then produce posters to display their learning. Density is covered in more detail in Chapter 8 of the *Complete Physics for Cambridge Secondary 1* Student book.

Activities
- Give two students identical bags. One is filled with heavy books, the other with lightly screwed-up paper. Which is heavier? Can students explain why? Tell students the heavier bag has the greater density. Density is how heavy something is for its size.
- Students measure the mass and volume of objects made from different materials, and calculate their densities. Include objects with cuboid shapes, so that students can calculate their volumes by measuring the lengths of their sides; also include objects with other shapes so that students can find their volumes by immersing in water in a measuring cylinder. **Worksheet 5.3.1** supports this activity.
- Student pairs find out about one factor that affects density – either particle mass, or how closely the particles are packed. Pairs plan how to teach other pairs what they have learnt. **Worksheet 5.3.2** and page 85 in the Student book support this activity.
- Pairs come together in fours, and teach each other about the factors that affect density. They summarise what they have learnt on a poster. **Worksheet 5.3.2** supports this activity.

Extension

Students read about the work of al-Biruni in the Student book, and further research his work on the Internet.

Homework

Workbook page 40

Key words

density, mass, volume, particle size

Student book, pages 86–87

CD resources

- Worksheet 5.4.1
- Worksheet 5.4.2
- Egg in a bottle animation

Objectives

- Explain what causes gas pressure
- Explain air pressure and its effect on boiling point
- Explain how temperature affects gas pressure

Overview

This lesson explains gas pressure in terms of colliding particles. It begins by looking at a balloon – why does it get bigger when inflated? What are the particles doing? There follows a fascinating demonstration, in which air pressure pushes a hard-boiled egg into a conical flask. The **egg in a bottle animation** on the CD-ROM shows what is happening to the steam and air particles during this experiment. Students then do the collapsing can experiment, and use ideas about particles to explain their observations. The lesson concludes by returning to the balloon – why does it get smaller when cooled in a fridge?

Activities

- Blow up a balloon. Ask why it gets bigger. Explain that air particles move inside it rapidly in all directions. They collide with the rubber and exert a force on it. The force per unit area is pressure. If possible, put the balloon in a fridge. Students predict how it will change. Part A of **worksheet 5.4.1** supports this activity.

- Demonstrate how air pressure pushes an egg into a flask: in a conical flask, heat 2 cm depth of water to boiling. Turn off the Bunsen burner. Place a hard-boiled egg (shell removed) in the neck of the flask. When the water vapour condenses, the gas pressure outside is greater than that inside. The egg drops into the flask. Part B of **worksheet 5.4.1** supports this activity.

- Students do the collapsing can experiment, and use ideas about particles to explain it. **Worksheet 5.4.2** supports this activity. The answer to question 1 is D, A, E, B, F, C.

- Return to the balloon in the fridge. How has it changed? Explain that it is smaller because the cooler air particles inside it move more slowly. They collide with each other, and the inside of the bottle, less often. The pressure inside has decreased. Part C of **worksheet 5.4.1** supports this activity.

Extension

Students use the Student book to find out about air pressure, and to explain why air pressure affects the boiling temperature of water.

Homework

Workbook page 41

Key words

collide, pressure, air pressure

Objective

- Understand how scientists use questions, evidence, and creative thought to develop explanations

Overview

This lesson, on ideas and evidence, focuses on the work of Robert Boyle and Robert Hooke in developing an explanation about the Torricelli barometer. It begins with a look at empirical questions – what are they? Can students write their own? This builds on the first activity of lesson 1.3.

Student groups then create short plays to describe the work of Boyle and Hooke, and to show how they created their explanation. The process of developing explanations is described in lesson 1.3, but this is the first time the role of creative thinking has been made explicit.

Activities

- Explain that scientific questions, also called empirical questions, are ones that evidence will help to answer. Student pairs make up some empirical questions of their own. Discuss some of these as a class.
- Students read about the work of Robert Boyle and Robert Hooke, making sure they fully understand the process of developing explanations that is given on page 89 of the Student book.
- In groups of four, students create short plays/dramas to describe the work of Boyle and Hooke, and to show how they developed their explanation. **Worksheets 5.5.1** and **5.5.2** support this activity.
- Student groups perform their plays to the class, and members of the audience suggest improvements.

Extension

Students use the Internet to find out more about the work of Boyle, Hooke, or Torricelli.

Homework

Workbook page 42

Key words

empirical question, creative thinking, prediction

CD resources
- Worksheet 5.6.1
- Worksheet 5.6.2

Objectives

Understand how to:
- plan an investigation
- obtain and present evidence
- consider evidence

Overview

In this lesson students plan and carry out an investigation to investigate the relationship between gas volume and temperature. They obtain evidence, and present it on a line graph. The lesson continues with a discussion about the evidence obtained. Does all the data fit the pattern, or are some of them anomalous? Finally, students are reminded of the term *correlation* (introduced in 5.2).

An alternative investigation (the one described in the Student book) that could be tackled during this lesson is described here *www.nuffieldfoundation.org/ practical-physics/thermal-expansion-air-charles-law*. However, the capillary tubing required is difficult to obtain.

Activities

- Refer back to the balloon of lesson 5.5. What happened to its volume when it cooled? Elicit that as temperature decreased, so did the volume.
- Take the apparatus shown on **worksheet 5.6.1**. Hold the flask in your hands to warm the air inside it. Show that oil moves up the tube as the air expands.
- Students plan a quantitative investigation based on the demonstration in the previous activity. They do the investigation and present the evidence on line graphs. **Worksheet 5.6.1** and **5.6.2** support this activity.
- Ask if any student has results that do not fit the pattern – these are anomalous. Discuss what to do about these results – ignore them? Repeat the investigation? Read page 91 of the Student book.
- Use the Student book graphs to reinforce the meaning of the term *correlation*. Read page 91 of the Student book.

Homework

Workbook page 43

Key words

correlation, anomalous, trend, pattern

CD resources
- Worksheet 6.1.1
- Worksheet 6.1.2

Objectives
- Explain what an element is
- Explain what an atom is
- Understand the importance of questions, evidence, and creative thought in developing explanations

Overview

In this lesson, students are reminded about elements. They then learn about atoms, and make posters to display what they know about elements and their atoms. Students then look at the development of ideas about atoms. Having read the section in the Student book, they create dramas to highlight the use of creative thought and evidence in developing explanations about atoms.

Activities
- Student pairs discuss what they know about atoms. What are they made up of? Has anyone heard of atoms? If possible, show students toy bricks and use them to model atoms, as shown on page 94 of the Student book.
- Students follow the guidance, and use information from page 94 of the Student book, to make posters to display their knowledge about atoms and elements. **Worksheet 6.1.1** supports this activity.
- Students read about the development of ideas about atoms in the Student book. In groups of at least four they create dramas to describe how early philosophers and scientists used creative thought and evidence in developing explanations about atoms. **Worksheet 6.1.2** supports this activity.
- Student groups perform their plays to the class, and members of the audience suggest improvements.

Extension

Students use the Internet to find out more about any of the philosophers or scientists in mentioned in the lesson.

Homework

Workbook page 44

Key words

atom, element, ideas, evidence

CD resources
- Worksheet 6.2.1
- Worksheet 6.2.2

Objectives
- Know the chemical symbols of the first twenty elements of the periodic table
- Understand why scientists use chemical symbols for elements

Overview
This lesson introduces chemical symbols. To start, students suggest reasons for elements having symbols. They then practise writing chemical symbols correctly, before playing games using element symbol and name cards. Students then use the periodic table to help them make up quiz questions about element names and chemical symbols. Finally, students swap with others and answer the quiz questions.

Activities
- Tell students that each element has its own chemical symbol. Ask student pairs to suggest why, and elicit that they are shorter to write and internationally understood. Read page 96 of the Student book.

- Students practise writing chemical symbols correctly by listing the first 20 elements and their symbols. Emphasise the correct use of lower and upper case letters. Read page 97 of the Student book.

- Students play games with the element name and symbol cards on **worksheets 6.2.1** and **6.2.2**, including memory and snap:
  - For memory, spread out the cards, face down, on the table. The first player turns over two cards. If they are a pair (element and symbol) the player keeps them and has another turn. If they are not a pair, the next player has a turn.
  - For snap, deal out the cards. Hold them face down. Players take turns to quickly turn over one card. When players spot a pair, they shout *snap*. First person to shout wins the pile.

- Students make up quiz questions on element names and chemical symbols, for example *Name four elements whose symbols start with S; name two elements named after countries*. Students swap quizzes and answer questions. Read page 97 of the Student book.

Homework
Workbook page 45

Key words
chemical symbol, element, periodic table

Student book, pages 98–99

CD resource
- Worksheet 6.3.1

Objective

- Understand some factors that influenced when elements were discovered

Overview

This lesson is about the discovery of elements, focusing on factors that influenced when different elements were first found. The lesson begins with an opportunity for students to speculate about which elements were discovered earliest. It continues with a group activity, in which students work together to find out about the elements discovered in different time periods. Student groups then create posters to summarise and display what they have learnt.

Activities

- Student pairs speculate about which elements were discovered earliest. Why do they think these elements were first found so long ago?

- Divide students into groups of four. These are *home groups*. Within home groups, each student is allocated one question from **worksheet 6.3.1**.

  Students doing the same question then get together in new groups of three or four. These are *expert groups*. Expert groups tackle the questions using information from the Student book, and plan how to teach their home groups what they have learnt.

  Students return to their home groups, and teach each other what they have learnt.

- Students remain in their home groups. They create posters or dramas to show what they have learnt about the discovery of elements.

- Home groups present their posters or dramas to one other group. The other group peer assesses. The final part of **worksheet 6.3.1** supports this activity.

Extension

Use the Internet to find out more about the discovery of particular elements. See *www.rsc.org/periodic-table* and *www.webelements.com*

Homework

Workbook page 46

Key words

elements, explanation, discovery, periodic table

♻ **CD resources**
- ■ Worksheet 6.4.1
- ■ Worksheet 6.4.2
- ■ Worksheet 6.4.3
- ■ Worksheet 6.4.4

Objective

- Explain how scientists asked questions, collected evidence, and thought creatively to develop the periodic table.

Overview

This lesson tells the story of one of the most important developments in chemistry – the discovery of the periodic table. Like lesson 6.1, it takes the form of group dramas. This time, though, students create television programmes to take viewers through the stages in some detail. Role cards are provided. The lesson finishes with a look at the development of theories in general, and a consideration of how the creation of the periodic table fits with this model.

Activities

- In groups of six, students read the guidance for the drama activity on **worksheet 6.4.1**, and clarify the task if necessary. They allocate individual roles.

- Students use their role cards to create and practise their group dramas. **Worksheets 6.4.2** and **6.4.3** support this activity.

- Student groups perform their dramas. Others use the peer assessment grid on **worksheet 6.4.4** to evaluate each one.

- Lead a description and discussion of the flow diagram on page 101 of the Student book showing how theories are created. Ask students to consider how the creation of the periodic table fits with this model.

Extension

Students use the Internet to find out more about any of the scientists in this lesson.

Homework

Workbook page 47

Key words

empirical question, evidence, explanation

CD resource
- Worksheet 6.5.1

Objective

- Practise interpreting secondary data

Overview

This lesson is an opportunity for students to practise interpreting secondary data. It begins with a reminder about primary and secondary sources. Students then plot melting point data for three groups of the periodic table. They describe patterns in the data, and compare the patterns for the three groups. Students then examine interpretations of density data made by others, and decide which interpretation is better. The lesson ends with a look at a pie chart – can students interpret this successfully?

Activities

- Remind students that primary data is that which they collect themselves, by making their own observations or measurements. Secondary data is data from others. Students may obtain secondary data from text books, data books, the Internet, or other students.

- Students follow the guidance on **worksheet 6.5.1** to draw bar charts to display the melting points of the elements of Groups 1, 7, and 0. They describe patterns in the data, and compare the patterns for the three groups. Do not allow students to look at pages 102–103 of the Student book during this activity.

- Students look at the density data in the table on page 103 of the Student book. They discuss the two interpretations given in the book, and decide which is better. A few groups justify their choice to the class.

- Students look at the pie chart on page 103 of the Student book. They answer questions 1 and 2 to practise interpreting data from pie charts.

Homework

Workbook page 48

Key words

group, secondary source, secondary data, patterns

CD resources
- Worksheet 6.6.1
- Inside copper animation

Objectives

- Describe differences between metals and non-metals
- Explain differences between metals and non-metals

Overview

This lesson begins with a reminder about the properties of typical metal and non-metal elements, covered in lessons 2.2 and 2.3. Students then look at models or diagrams of atom arrangements in typical metals and non-metals. The lesson continues with a group activity in which students work together to use atom arrangements to explain metal and non-metal properties. Finally, students check their learning by answering the questions in the Student book.

The **inside copper animation** on the CD-ROM shows how the arrangement of atoms in copper explain its properties.

Activities

- Display samples of metal and non-metal elements. Non-metals could include carbon (as charcoal), sulfur, and sealed jars labelled *oxygen*, *nitrogen*, and *hydrogen*. Elicit differences in the properties of typical metals and non-metals. Students should refer to the table on page 104 of the Student book.

- Use models to show the atom arrangements in typical metal and non-metal elements, or display the diagrams on page 105 of the Student book.

- Divide students into groups of four. Within each group, allocate one pair to do each question on the **worksheet 6.6.1**. These pairs are called *sub-groups*.

  Sub-groups tackle the questions using information from page 105 of the Student book, and plan how to teach the rest of their group what they have learnt.

  Within each group, sub-groups teach each other what they have learnt.

- To check their learning, students answer the questions on page 105 of the Student book.

Homework

Workbook page 49

Key words

molecule, metal, non-metal, properties, atom arrangement

CD resources

- Worksheet 6.7.1
- Worksheet 6.7.2

Objectives

- Understand what a compound is
- Give examples of compounds and state how their properties are different from the properties of their elements

Overview

This lesson introduces compounds. It begins with a demonstration to show that the properties of a compound are very different from those of the elements it is made up of. Students then explore the properties of iron, sulfur, and iron sulfide, and note their differences. Finally, students use models to show that compounds are made up of atoms of more than one element, strongly joined together. At this stage, to avoid misconceptions, it is best to model only simple molecular compounds.

Activities

- If possible, display three substances – sodium, chlorine (in a gas jar), and sodium chloride (as table salt). Tell students that sodium chloride is made up of two elements, sodium and chlorine. Sodium chloride is an example of a compound. Give a second example of a compound, calcium phosphate. Use page 106 of the Student book to describe how the properties of the compound are different from the properties of the elements it is made up of.
- Students do two practicals to explore the properties of iron, sulfur, and iron sulfide. **Worksheet 6.7.1** and **6.7.2** support this activity.
- Use models to show that compounds are made up of atoms of more than one element, strongly joined together. Suitable examples include carbon monoxide, carbon dioxide, and water. If possible, allow students to make models using toy bricks or molecular model kits.

Extension

Students use the Internet to research differences in properties between compounds and the elements they are made up of.

Homework

Workbook page 50

Key words

compound, atom, element

CD resources
- Worksheet 6.8.1
- Worksheet 6.8.2

Objective

- Understand the stages involved in an enquiry

Overview

The lesson starts with a demonstration to show that, when iron is heated in air, the mass increases since iron joins with oxygen to make a compound. Students then do their own investigations into the mass change when magnesium burns in oxygen. They compare their results with those of other groups, and suggest improvements to the investigation.

Activities

- Demonstrate the investigation shown in the Student book, emphasising the investigation stages described in the book. Full details of the investigation are given at *www.nuffieldfoundation.org/practical-chemistry/combustion-iron-wool*

- Students investigate the mass change involved in the combustion reaction of magnesium. **Worksheet 6.8.1** and **6.8.2** give guidance on selecting ideas to test, controlling risk, making a prediction, making measurements, obtaining evidence, doing simple calculations, and making a conclusion.

- Gather together results from all groups. Student pairs speculate on reasons for the different values obtained, and suggest improvements to the investigation.

Homework

Workbook page 51

Key words

hazard, risk

Student book, pages 110–111

CD resource
- Worksheet 6.9.1

Objectives

- Name compounds
- Write and interpret formulae

Overview

In this lesson students learn how to name compounds, and how to write and interpret formulae. The lesson begins with an introduction to the idea that names give clues about the elements that make up a compound. For example, a name ending in *–ate* shows that the compound includes oxygen atoms. Students then use models to help them understand how to name compounds made up of atoms of non-metal elements only. Finally, students learn how to write formulae. They practise writing and interpreting formulae for molecular elements, and compounds.

Activities

- Show students four compounds – sodium chloride, copper oxide, copper sulfate, and copper carbonate. They guess which elements make up the compounds. Explain that compounds whose names end in *–ide* include atoms of just one non-metal; compounds whose names end in *–ate* include atoms of oxygen and another non-metal. Students do the questions on Part A of **worksheet 6.9.1**.

- Display molecular models of compounds made up of atoms of non-metals only, including carbon monoxide, carbon dioxide, sulfur dioxide, and sulfur trioxide. Explain how the compounds are named. Students do Part B of **worksheet 6.9.1** on naming compounds.

- Students make models of the elements or compounds shown in the first table on page 111 of the Student book. They then do Part C of **worksheet 6.9.1** on writing and interpreting formulae.

Homework

Workbook page 52

Key words

formula, compounds, chemical symbols

CD resources
- Worksheet 6.10.1
- Worksheet 6.10.2
- Worksheet 6.10.3

Objectives

- Name some common oxides and hydroxides
- Describe one difference in the properties of metal oxides and non-metal oxides

Overview

In this lesson students explore the properties of oxides of metals and non-metals, and find out that non-metal oxides are acidic and metal oxides are basic. Students also learn that some metal hydroxides dissolve in water to make alkaline solutions. The lesson continues with a look at the formulae of common oxides and hydroxides. Finally, students use the Student book or the Internet to research the properties and uses of some common oxides, hydroxides, sulfates, and carbonates, and create posters to communicate what they have found out.

Activities

- Display samples of three oxides – magnesium oxide, calcium oxide, and copper oxide. Students speculate what they have in common. They do a practical using **worksheet 6.10.1** to find out that they are bases – they neutralise acids, and if they dissolve in water the solution will be alkaline. Students also measure the pH of sodium hydroxide solution, and learn that it is alkaline.
- Students follow the guidance on **worksheet 6.10.2** to find out that non-metal oxides are acidic.
- Students write formulae for oxides and hydroxides. Part A of **worksheet 6.10.3** supports this activity.
- Students use the Student book or the Internet to research the properties and uses of some oxides, hydroxides, sulfates, and carbonate. They create posters to communicate what they have found out. Part B of **worksheet 6.10.3** supports this activity.

Homework

Workbook page 53

Key words

oxide, bases, hydroxide, sulfate, carbonate

Student book, pages 114–115

CD resources

- Worksheet 6.11.1
- Worksheet 6.11.2

Objective

- Plan investigations, present evidence, and consider the evidence

Overview

This lesson focuses on enquiry skills. Through part-planning and carrying out an investigation to find the percentage by mass of salt in sea water, students practise the skills of selecting ideas to test, controlling risk, taking accurate measurements, using equipment correctly, making simple calculations, and making a conclusion.

If sea water is not available, make a substitute by dissolving about 35 g of sodium chloride in 1 dm^3 (one litre) of tap water. The investigation gives better results, and is safer, if the solution is heated to remove most water, but then left in a warm, dry place for the remaining water to evaporate slowly.

Activities

- Display some table salt (sodium chloride). Elicit that the salt is sodium chloride, $NaCl$. We obtain most of it from sea water or rock salt. Pairs discuss how much salt is in the sea.

- Ask how we could find the percentage by mass of salt in sea water. Elicit that we could take a known mass of seawater, evaporate the water, and find the mass of solute remaining. Most – but not all – the solute is sodium chloride.

- Students plan and do an investigation to find the percentage by mass of salt in sea water. **Worksheets 6.11.1** and **6.11.2** support this activity.

- Gather results from all groups. Students speculate on reasons for differences, and suggest improvements to the investigation.

Extension

Students use the Internet to find out more about salts in the oceans, and their different total concentration in different regions. This web page is a useful starting point:

www.seafriends.org.nz/oceano/seawater.htm#salinity

Homework

Workbook page 54

Key words

chloride, meniscus

Student book, pages 116–117

CD resource
- Worksheet 6.12.1

Objective

- Understand the differences between elements, mixtures, and compounds

Overview

This lesson introduces mixtures. It starts with a discussion about familiar mixtures, for example sea water, air, and fruit juice. How are mixtures different from compounds? Students then plan and do a practical to separate salt from rock salt. Some groups then justify their choice of separation techniques to the class. The lesson concludes with an opportunity for students to check their learning by answering the Student book questions.

If rock salt is not available, make a substitute by mixing sand, table salt, and a few small stones. It is safer to perform the evaporation stage by heating the salt solution to remove most of the water, and then leaving in a warm, dry place for the remaining water to evaporate slowly.

Activities

- Tell students that sea water, air, and fruit juice are all mixtures. A mixture may contain elements, compounds, or both. The substances in a mixture are not chemically joined together. Elicit further differences between mixtures and compounds. The table on page 117 of the Student book summarises the differences between mixtures and compounds.

- Students plan and do a practical to separate salt from rock salt. This practical experiment will review what they know about mixtures from Primary level. They list the stages they use – and the reason for each stage – on **worksheet 6.12.1**. The best order for the processes listed is dissolving, filtering, evaporating.

- Students display their samples of salt. A few groups tell the rest of the class what they did, and why. They can base what they say on their completed planning sheets.

- Students check their understanding by answering the questions on page 117 of the Student book.

Homework

Workbook page 55

Key words

mixture, elements, compounds, ratio

Student book, pages 118–119

CD resource

■ Worksheet 6.13.1

Objective

● Describe how to separate mixtures by decanting and filtering

Overview

This lesson focuses on two separation techniques – filtering and decanting. The focus of the lesson is different from that in the Student book, which concentrates on enquiry methods.

The lesson starts with a brief demonstration of decanting, in which cooking oil is separated from a mixture with water. Students then plan presentations and demonstrations for primary school students on decanting and filtering. Their presentations should include explanations of why each technique works. The lesson finishes with performances of the presentations, and a peer assessment for each group. *The activities on this page review the work on* Separating Mixtures *that students will have done as part of the Cambridge Primary curriculum framework.*

Activities

● Show students a mixture of recently-shaken cooking oil and water. Pairs discuss how to separate the mixture. Elicit that the process of decanting can be used, and demonstrate this.

● Students follow the guidance to plan presentations for primary school students on filtering and decanting. The presentations should include demonstrations, and explanations of why each technique works. **Worksheet 6.13.1** supports this activity.

● Student groups present their presentation to one other group. The other group peer assesses using the criteria on the final part of **worksheet 6.13.1**.

Homework

Workbook page 56

Key words

decant, filter, filtration

Student book, pages 120–121

CD resources
- Worksheet 6.14.1
- Worksheet 6.14.2

Objective

- Understand how evaporation and distillation separate liquids and solids from solutions

Overview

This lesson continues the theme of separating mixtures, started in lesson 6.12. It begins with a brief reminder about separating salt from its solution in water by evaporation. It continues with a demonstration of distillation, in which a solvent is separated from its solution by evaporation and condensation. Students then do a simple distillation procedure themselves. The lesson finishes with a brief mention of one of the first scientists to use distillation, Jabir ibn Hayyan. This lesson reviews some material that students will have covered as part of the Primary Science curriculum framework. Encourage students to think about how the different properties of materials affect how mixtures can be separated. *The activities on this page review the work on* Separating Mixtures *that students will have done as part of the Cambridge Primary curriculum framework.*

Activities

- Show students some seawater. Ask if they would like to drink it. Remind them that they can obtain salt from sea water by evaporation, but how can they obtain pure water? The next activity shows how.

- Use the apparatus shown on the **worksheet 6.14.1** to demonstrate obtaining pure water from a mixture of ink and water by distillation. This mixture has been chosen since it is easy to see that ink-free water is produced. Students label the diagram on the worksheet. Tell students that a version of distillation is used in desalination, to produce pure water from sea water on a large scale in places with low rainfall.

- Students follow the guidance on **worksheet 6.14.2** to obtain pure water from ink solution.

- Tell students that Jabir ibn Hayyan was one of the first scientists to use distillation. He lived in the Middle East from 721–815.

Extension

Students use the Internet to find out more about Jabir's work on distillation.

Homework

Workbook page 57

Key words

evaporation, distillation

Student book, pages 122–123

CD resource
- Worksheet 6.15.1

Objective

- Explain how fractional distillation separates mixtures of liquids with different boiling points

Overview

This extension lesson introduces the technique of fractional distillation as a way of separating mixtures of liquids with different boiling points. It begins with a simple demonstration of the fractional distillation of a crude oil substitute. It continues with student explanations – what is fractional distillation, and how does it work?

Activities

- Ask students about vehicle fuels. Where do diesel and petrol come from? Elicit that both come from crude oil. Crude oil is a mixture of compounds. Elicit that the compounds can be separated by distillation.

- Demonstrate the simple fractional distillation of a crude oil substitute. Use the apparatus, and follow the procedure, shown on **worksheet 6.15.1**. Demonstrate the viscosity and flammability of the fractions, and ask students to identify trends in these properties.

- Students read about fractional distillation on pages 122–3 of the Student book. In pairs they plan illustrated talks in which they use ideas about changes of state to explain how fractional distillation works. Their talks could draw on one of two examples – the fractional distillation of an ethanol/water mixture, or of crude oil.

- Student pairs give their talks to other pairs, and suggest improvements.

Homework

Workbook page 58

Key words

fractional distillation, crude oil, fractionating column

Student book, pages 124–125

CD resources
- Worksheet 6.16.1
- Worksheet 6.16.2

Objectives

- Understand how chromatography separates mixtures
- Give examples of uses of chromatography

Overview

This lesson shows how chromatography can be used to separate mixtures of dyes from pens and leaves. It begins with a scene-setter – how can you tell whether green marks on a criminal's T-shirt are from grass, spinach, or cassava leaves? To solve this problem, students first try out the technique of chromatography to separate the dyes from ink samples. They then plan and do an investigation in which they use chromatography to answer the question posed at the start of the lesson.

Activities

- Display a piece of cloth with green stains on it. Tell students that police need to know whether the stains are from grass, spinach, or cassava leaves. Set the challenge – students will use chromatography to identify the source of the green stains.

- Students follow the guidance on **worksheet 6.16.1** to experience chromatography by making chromatograms of ink samples, ideally from felt-tip pens.

- Students plan and do an investigation to identify the source of the green stains introduced in activity 1. Discuss the results as a class – how sure can you be that the conclusions are correct? **Worksheet 6.16.2** supports this activity – each group needs a strip of chromatography paper with a spot of spinach on the pencil line.

- Students read about some uses of chromatography, focusing on the study on cassava described on page 125 of the Student book.

Homework

Workbook page 59

Key words

chromatography, chromatogram, empirical question, evidence, explanation

Student book, pages 126–127

CD resource
■ Worksheet 6.17.1

Objectives

- Describe how to separate metals from ores
- Calculate the mass of metal obtained from an ore sample

Overview

In this lesson students use ideas about separation techniques to explain how tin is extracted from its ore. The main activity is a group activity, in which students work together to answer three questions about the extraction of tin from its ore: How does tin exist naturally, and where is it found? How is tin oxide separated from the substances it is mixed with in its ore? What chemical reaction is used to obtain tin from tin oxide, and how is this tin separated from the impurities it is mixed with? Student groups then create posters to demonstrate what they have learnt.

Activities

- Use the Student book to help explain how gold is obtained by panning. Point out that this technique only works for metals that exist naturally as elements on their own. The extraction of other metals – such as tin – requires a greater number of steps.

- Divide students into groups of three. These are *home groups*. Within home groups, each student is allocated one question from **worksheet 6.17.1**.

  Students doing the same question then get together in new groups of three or four. These are *expert groups*. Expert groups tackle the questions using information from page 126 of the Student book, and plan how to teach their home groups what they have learnt.

  Students return to their home groups, and teach each other what they have learnt.

- Students remain in home groups. They create posters to demonstrate what they have learnt about extracting tin from its ore.

- Home groups present their posters to one other group. The other group peer assesses. Part 5 of **worksheet 6.17.1** supports this activity.

Homework

Workbook page 60

Key words

ore, panning, filtration, tin

Student book, pages 128–129

CD resource
- Worksheet 6.18.1

Objective
- Name the main elements in living things

Overview
This lesson is about the elements of life. It begins with a look at the human body – what are the main elements in us? Where do they come from? Students create posters to address these questions. Students then find out about iodine deficiency. They create radio or television programmes to describe an iodine deficiency disease, and to tell others about a study in which scientists researched the impact of action taken to prevent iodine deficiency diseases in Tanzania.

Activities
- Ask students to guess the main elements that make up their own bodies. Use information from page 128 of the Student book to give the answer. Pairs produce posters to show the main elements in a human body, and also to show where they come from.
- Students read about iodine deficiency in the Student book. In groups of four, they use **worksheet 6.18.1** to help them create a radio or television programme to tell others about iodine deficiency, and about the Tanzanian study described in the Student book.
- Student groups perform their programmes to at least one other group. The listening/viewing groups evaluate the programmes according to the criteria at the bottom of the **worksheet 6.18.1**.

Extension
Use the Internet to research one other deficiency disease.

Homework
Workbook page 61

Key words
vitamin, mineral, inverse correlation, deficiency

CD resources

- Worksheet 7.1.1
- Worksheet 7.1.2
- Worksheet 7.1.3

Objectives

- Know what chemical reactions are
- Know how to recognise chemical reactions

Overview

The lesson starts with two short demonstrations to introduce the idea of chemical reactions. Students then carry out their own reactions, and notice signs that may indicate that a reaction is occurring. They then burn magnesium in air, and are introduced to the terms *reactant* and *product*.

Activities

- Demonstrate frying an egg. Then demonstrate another chemical reaction – add one spatula of potassium thiocyanate to about 50 cm^3 of water to dissolve, followed by a few drops of 0.1 mol/dm^3 iron(III) chloride. Deep red iron thiocyanate forms.

- Students follow the guidance on **worksheets 7.1.1** and **7.1.2** to carry out their own chemical reactions.

- Lead a discussion to elicit some signs of chemical reactions, including temperature changes, sounds, smells, and flames. Then define chemical reactions as changes which create new substances and cannot be reversed. Read page 132 of the Student book. **Worksheet 7.1.2** supports this activity.

- Demonstrate burning magnesium in air. Students should observe the experiment carefully. Introduce the terms *combustion, reactant,* and *product*. **Worksheet 7.1.3** supports this activity.

Extension

Students do further research about burning reactions, including finding interesting examples.

Homework

Workbook page 62

Key words

reactants, products, combustion, burning

CD resources

- Worksheet 7.2.1
- Worksheet 7.2.2
- Worksheet 7.2.3

Objective

- Write word equations to represent chemical reactions

Overview

The purpose of this lesson is for students to learn how to write word equations to represent chemical reactions simply. During the lesson, students carry out five chemical reactions. They record their observations. Having been told the names of the reactants and products, students write word equations for each of their reactions.

During the lesson, emphasise that the meaning of the arrow in chemical equations is different from the meaning of the equals sign in maths. Also make clear that you cannot guess the names of products of reactions.

Activities

- On the board, write a sentence to describe a chemical reaction, for example *magnesium reacts with oxygen from the air to make one product, magnesium oxide*. Tell students they can summarise the reaction using just four words by writing a word equation.

- Students follow the guidance on **worksheets 7.2.1** and **7.2.2** to carry out five chemical reactions and record their observations.

- As a class, discuss the observations of the chemical reactions. Give the names of the reactants and products for each reaction. Students then write word equations for each reaction. The products are: 1 – iron oxide; 2 – iron hydroxide and sodium chloride; 3 – sodium ethanoate, carbon dioxide, and water; 4 – zinc chloride and hydrogen; 5 – copper sulfate and water. **Worksheet 7.2.3** supports this activity.

- Students complete the questions on Part 3 of **worksheet 7.2.3** to practise writing word equations.

Homework

Workbook page 63

Key words

word equation, neutralisation, salt, reaction

Student book, pages 136–137

CD resource
- Worksheet 7.3.1

Objectives

- Understand what corrosion is
- Know how to prevent iron corroding

Overview

This lesson is about corrosion. It begins with an opportunity for students to share what they already know about rusting and corrosion. It continues with a group activity, in which students work together to answer three key questions: What makes iron corrode? Why is the corrosion of iron – and other metals – a problem? How can iron corrosion be prevented? Student groups then create posters to summarise and display what they have learnt.

The study of corrosion continues in lesson 7.4, in which students carry out an investigation.

Activities

- Student pairs discuss what they already know about corrosion, including the rusting of iron. A few pairs feedback.
- Divide students into groups of three. These are *home groups*. Within home groups, each student is allocated one question from **worksheet 7.3.1**.

  Students doing the same question then get together in new groups of three or four. These are *expert groups*. Expert groups tackle the questions using information from pages 136-7 of the Student book, and plan how to teach their home groups what they have learnt.

  Students return to their home groups, and teach each other what they have learnt.

- Students remain in home groups. They create posters to show what they have learnt about corrosion.
- Home groups present their posters to one other group. The other group peer assesses using the grid at the bottom of **worksheet 7.3.1**.

Extension

Students do further research about burning reactions, including finding interesting examples.

Homework

Workbook page 64

Key words

corrosion, rusting

CD resources

- Worksheet 7.4.1
- Worksheet 7.4.2

Objective

- Reinforce the stages of doing an investigation

Overview

This lesson continues the work on corrosion started in lesson 7.3. It is designed to reinforce the stages in planning and carrying out an investigation. Students spend the lesson planning and setting up their investigation, and predicting results. They will need to examine the results of their investigation, and consider the evidence obtained, one week later.

Possible investigation questions are given in the Student book. The Workbook also gives an example of a suitable investigation.

Activities

- Tell students that they will today plan and set up an investigation about corrosion. Discuss what they can remember about this topic from lesson 7.3. If possible show a brief video clip about corrosion, for example that at: *www.bbc.co.uk/learningzone/clips/rusting-of-iron-process-and-prevention/1856.html*

- Students follow the guidance on **worksheet 7.4.1** and **7.4.2** to plan and set up an investigation. Encourage them to read carefully pages 138–9 in the Student book – and, if possible, page 65 of the Workbook – to help inform their choice of investigation question.

- Finish the lesson by discussing students' predictions. How confident are they in these?

Extension

Students use the Internet to further research some implications of corrosion. *www.corrosion.org* has some interesting videos about the topic.

Homework

Workbook page 65

Key words

questions, evidence, secondary sources

Student book, pages 140–141

⊘ **CD resources**
- Worksheet 7.5.1
- Worksheet 7.5.2

Objective

- Know how to use chemical reactions to identify metal elements in compounds

Overview

In this extension lesson, students witness the flame colours made by compounds of different elements. They are introduced to two applications of this phenomenon – identifying unknown compounds, and making fireworks. Students then observe the coloured precipitates formed when sodium hydroxide solution is added to different metal salts. They write word equations for the reactions observed, and find out how this method can be used to identify compounds.

Activities

- If possible, show a video clip of fireworks. Suitable clips can be found by searching the Internet for *firework video*.

- Students follow the guidance on **worksheet 7.5.1** to perform flame tests on salts of the following metals: lithium, sodium, potassium, calcium, and barium. As a class, discuss how flame tests can be used to help identify unknown compounds.

- Students follow the guidance on **worksheet 7.5.2** to make precipitates of metal hydroxides. As a class, discuss how this method can be used to help identify unknown compounds.

- Students write word equations for the precipitation reactions they have observed. Students should complete the questions on **worksheet 7.5.2**.

Homework

Workbook page 66

Key words

flame test, precipitate

CD resources
- Worksheet 8.1.1
- Worksheet 8.1.2
- Worksheet 8.1.3
- 8.1. The atom illustration

Objectives
- Name the three sub-atomic particles, and describe their properties
- Describe the structure of an atom

Overview
This lesson introduces students to sub-atomic particles and atomic structure. Students learn the mass and charge of each sub-atomic particle, and that the nucleus is made up of protons and neutrons. In a neutral atom, the numbers of protons and electrons are equal.

The illustration from page 146 of the Student book is included on the CD-ROM with and without labels. This could be used as plenary activity to find out what students already know about atoms.

The arrangement of electrons in shells around the nucleus is covered in lesson 8.4.

Activities
- Show students about ten small identical balls. Each one represents an atom of the element helium. Discuss how the balls can be used to explain changes of state and diffusion. Tell students that the solid atom model cannot explain everything in chemistry, for example reactions. A new model is needed.

- Describe an atom as consisting of tiny sub-atomic particles. Protons and neutrons make up the nucleus. Electrons move around outside the nucleus. Atoms are electrically neutral because the number of protons is equal to the number of electrons. This model can be used to explain chemical reactions, and how atoms join together. **Worksheet 8.1.1** supports this activity.

- **Practical activity:** Explain that every atom of a certain element has the same number of protons. Student pairs use beans to model atomic structures of given atoms. At this stage they do not arrange electrons in shells, but simply spread them out around the outside of the nucleus. Students draw their models. **Worksheet 8.1.2** supports this activity.

Extension
Students tackle the questions on the sizes and masses of atoms, nuclei, and sub-atomic particles on **worksheet 8.1.3**.

Homework
Workbook page 67

Key words
sub-atomic particles, protons, neutrons, electrons, nucleus

Student book, pages 148–149

CD resources
- Worksheet 8.2.1
- Worksheet 8.2.2

Objective

- Describe how scientists work using historical examples

Overview

This lesson describes the contributions of two scientists to the development of models of atomic structure. Students first explore how J. J. Thomson used experimentation, evidence, and creative thought to discover electrons. They then make physical models to represent the models of atomic structure developed by Thomson and Nagaoka. Finally, students script a conversation in which Thomson and Nagaoka discuss and compare their models.

Activities

- Describe to students how Thomson explored cathode rays. Use the diagram to explain how he used experimentation, evidence, and creative thought to discover that cathode rays are negatively charged. Read from page 148 of the Student book.

- Students complete the diagram on **worksheet 8.2.1** to show how Thomson discovered that electrons are particles that are part of atoms. Higher attaining students can complete the diagram in their own words; students can also write phrases from the bottom of the sheet in the correct boxes on the diagram.

- **Practical activity:** Students make physical models to represent Thomson's plum pudding model and Nagaoka's Saturn model. Use beans or stones to represent electrons, and clay or dough to represent the positive parts of the atoms. Read from page 149 of the Student book.

- Student pairs script – and then perform – imaginary conversations in which Thomson and Nagaoka compare their models. The writing frame on **worksheet 8.2.2** supports this activity.

Extension

Explore the history of the discovery of the electron in more detail. This website is a useful starting point: *www.aip.org/history/electron/jjhome.htm*

Homework

Workbook page 68

Key words

nucleus, electrons, model

CD resources

- Worksheet 8.3.1
- Worksheet 8.3.2
- Worksheet 8.3.3

Objective

- Describe the method and discoveries of Rutherford

Overview

This lesson describes how Rutherford and his colleagues, Geiger and Marsden, discovered the nucleus. The lesson begins with a description of the scientists' experiment, in which the scientists fired positively-charged particles at gold foil. Students then model one aspect of the experiment themselves. They next complete a comic strip, imagining conversations between the scientists as they do the experiment and later explain it. Finally, students are introduced to the neutron.

Activities

- Tell students that Rutherford wanted to test Thomson's plum pudding model. He worked with colleagues to do an experiment to gather evidence. Use the Student book to describe the experiment, or show an animation. **Worksheet 8.3.1** supports this activity.

- **Practical activity:** As a class, model the experiment as follows. Tie a piece of string to a large ball. Suspend it from the ceiling, or a tree. This represents a nucleus. Students throw small balls (or screwed-up pieces of paper) at the big ball. These represent positively-charged particles. Most small balls do not change direction. A few hit the nucleus and change direction. **Worksheet 8.3.2** supports this activity.

- Students add text to speech bubbles on the comic strip on **worksheet 8.3.3** to describe and explain the results of the Geiger-Marsden experiment.

- Students read the section *Inside the nucleus* from page 151 of the Student book. This introduces protons and neutrons.

Extension

Use the Internet to find out more about the discovery of the neutron. Go to *cambridgephysics.org* and click on the browse icon.

Homework

Workbook page 69

Key words

nucleus, electrons, model

Student book, pages 152–153

CD resources
- Worksheet 8.4.1
- Worksheet 8.4.2
- Worksheet 8.4.3

Objectives

- Draw the structures of atoms of the first twenty elements
- Describe patterns in the structures of these atoms

Overview

This lesson introduces electronic structure. Students use beans to show the electronic structures of atoms of different elements, and draw the electronic structures of these elements. They then draw the electronic structures of elements in the same group of the periodic table, and look for patterns in these structures.

Activities

- Remind students that the nucleus of an atom is made up of protons and neutrons, and that all atoms of an element have the same number of protons. In a neutral atom, the number of protons is equal to the number of electrons.

- **Practical activity:** Tell students that electrons occupy shells in atoms. Students use beans to model the electronic structures of atoms. They draw the arrangements, and then write the electronic structures in the form 2,8,1 and so on. **Worksheet 8.4.1** supports this activity.

- **Worksheet 8.4.2:** Students draw the electronic structures of atoms of the first three elements of Group 1 of the periodic table. They repeat for Groups 2 and 0, and look for patterns.

- **Worksheet 8.4.3:** Teacher reads out statements about electronic structure. Students show thumbs up for true statements, thumbs down for false statements, and thumbs horizontal if they are not sure.

Extension

Use the Internet to find out about the similarities in properties of the Group 1 elements, in preparation for lesson 8.6. Begin by searching online for *BBC Bitesize Group 1*.

Homework

Workbook page 70

Key words

shells, energy levels, orbits, electronic structure, protons, electrons

CD resources
- Worksheet 8.5.1
- Worksheet 8.5.2
- Worksheet 8.5.3

Objectives

- Work out the proton number and nucleon number of an atom
- Explain what isotopes are

Overview

This lesson introduces proton number and nucleon number, and links the concept of proton number to the periodic table. Students model atoms with different proton and nucleon numbers, and use a periodic table to identify them. They then do calculations linking proton number, nucleon number, and number of neutrons. Finally, students are introduced to the idea of isotopes. They make human models of isotopes before calculating the numbers of neutrons in different isotopes of an element.

Activities

- Explain that proton number is the number of protons in an atom of an element. Then explain that protons and neutrons are both nucleons, and that the number of nucleons in the nucleus of an atom is its nucleon number.
- **Practical activity:** Students use beans or bottle tops to model atoms given their proton and nucleon numbers. They then use the periodic table to identify the elements the atoms are from. **Worksheet 8.5.1** supports this activity.
- Students do the calculations linking proton number, nucleon number, and number of neutrons on **worksheet 8.5.2**.
- Explain that isotopes are atoms of the same element with different numbers of neutrons. Students take the role of protons and neutrons, to model three hydrogen isotopes. They then calculate the numbers of neutrons in different isotopes of an element. **Worksheet 8.5.3** supports this activity.

Homework

Workbook page 71

Key words

proton number, nucleon, nucleon number, mass number

Student book, pages 156–157

CD resources

- Worksheet 8.6.1
- Worksheet 8.6.2
- Worksheet 8.6.3

Objective

- Describe trends in properties of the Group 1 elements

Overview

In this lesson, students observe the reactions of the Group 1 elements with water, either as a teacher demonstration or on video clips. They use ideas about electronic structure to explain why the reactions are similar. Students then work in groups to find out about trends in the physical properties of the elements.

Activities

- **Practical activity:** Locate Group 1 in the periodic table. Then demonstrate the reactions of lithium, sodium, and potassium with water, or show video clips of the reactions. Students complete **worksheet 8.6.1**. For demonstration instructions go to *www.nuffieldfoundation.org/practical-chemistry* and search for *Group 1*. For video clips, search YouTube for *sodium and water*.

- Divide students into groups of 4. These are *home groups*. Within the home groups, each student is allocated one question from **worksheet 8.6.2**.

  Students doing the same question then get together in new groups of 4. These are *expert groups*. Each expert group tackles its question using the data on **worksheet 8.6.3**, and plans how to teach home groups what they have learnt.

  Students return to their home groups, and teach each other what they have learnt.

- Students remain in home groups. Teacher asks a few questions about trends in the physical properties of the Group 1 elements, to check learning from the previous activity.

Extension

Use the Internet to research the uses of Group 1 elements and their compounds. These websites are good places to begin: *rsc.org/periodic-table* and *webelements.com*

Homework

Workbook page 72

Key words

group, patterns, properties, trend, metal

CD resource
- Worksheet 8.7.1

Objective

- Describe trends in the properties of the Group 2 elements

Overview

In this lesson, students use electronic structures to explain why the properties of the Group 2 elements are similar. They then use their knowledge of the trends of the reactions of the Group 1 elements with water to predict a trend for Group 2. Next, students react calcium and magnesium with cold water, to test their prediction. They also learn how to test for hydrogen gas.

Activities

- Locate Group 2 in the periodic table. Students write the electronic structures of the elements in the form 2,8,2. Guide them to explain that all Group 2 elements have two electrons in their outermost shell. This is why their reactions are similar.

- **Practical activity:** Students use their knowledge of Group 1 reactions to predict the trend in the reactions of Group 2 elements with water. They test their prediction by reacting magnesium and calcium with cold water. **Worksheet 8.7.1** supports this activity.

- **Practical activity:** Students react calcium with cold water again, and test the gas given off to show that it is hydrogen (a lighted splint held in the gas will go out with a squeaky pop). Use the guidelines on page 234 of the Student book.

- Students consider the reactions of the Group 2 elements with acids, and answer question 3 on page 159 of the Student book to suggest how to compare the vigour of the reactions of beryllium and magnesium with hydrochloric acid.

Extension

Use the Internet to research the uses of Group 2 elements and their compounds. These websites are good places to begin: *rsc.org/periodic-table* and *webelements.com*

Homework

Workbook page 73

Key words

group, properties, pattern, trend, reaction

Student book, pages 160–161

CD resources
- Worksheet 8.8.1
- Worksheet 8.8.2

Objective

- Describe trends in the properties of Group 7 elements

Overview

In this lesson, students examine the physical properties of the halogens, and model their molecular structure. They then watch videos showing the reactions of the halogens with iron wool, and consider their hazards. They also write equations for the reactions.

Activities

- Locate Group 7 in the periodic table. Student pairs discuss what they know about the elements in this group, and then read the section *Deadly elements* on page 160 of the Student book.

- Students plot the melting points and boiling points of the halogens on a number line, and use this to answer questions about their states at different temperatures. Questions 1 and 2 on **worksheet 8.8.1** support this activity.

- **Practical activity:** Make models of halogen molecules, using matchsticks and plasticine, or students holding hands in pairs. Explain that elements that exist as molecules, like the halogens, are often gases; unlike most metals, which do not exist as molcules.

- Students read the section *Reactions of the Group 7 elements* in the Student book. Show videos of the reactions of the halogens with iron – search YouTube for *halogens iron wool*. **Worksheet 8.8.2** supports this activity.

Extension

Use the Internet to research the uses of Group 7 elements and their compounds. These websites are good places to begin: *rsc.org/periodic-table* and *webelements.com*

Homework

Workbook page 74

Key words

halogen, trend, properties, pattern, non-metal

CD resource
- Worksheet 8.9.1

Objective

- Look critically at sources of secondary data

Overview

Students begin by finding out about the history of adding chlorine and its compounds to drinking water. They make a small poster to summarise what they learn. Students then read about a scientific study on the effects of chlorinating water. In groups they create, perform, and evaluate a radio programme to tell listeners about the study and its findings.

Activities

- Students read about the history of adding chlorine and its compounds to drinking water. They make small illustrated posters to summarise their findings. Read from pages 162–3 of the Student book.

- Students read about a scientific study on the effects of chlorinating water. In groups of three, they use **worksheet 8.9.1** to help them create a radio programme to tell listeners about the study and its findings.

- Student groups perform their radio programmes to at least one other group. The listening groups evaluate the programmes according to the criteria at the bottom of **worksheet 8.9.1**.

Extension

Use the Internet to research the chlorination of drinking water in more detail. Start by looking at *worldchlorine.org* and navigating to publications.

Homework

Workbook page 75

Key words

chlorine, secondary data, evidence

CD resources

- Worksheet 8.10.1
- Worksheet 8.10.2

Objectives

- Describe trends in periods of the periodic table
- Describe patterns in data

Overview

Students begin by colouring in different groups and periods of the periodic table, for easy identification. They then plot bar charts of the melting points of the elements of periods 4 and 5 from secondary data, and identify any trends. They then compare these trends to those of periods 2 and 3 that are described in the Student book.

Activities

- Students colour in different groups and periods on the periodic table on **worksheet 8.10.1**.

- Students use data given on **worksheet 8.10.2** to plot bar charts of the melting points of the elements of periods 4 and 5. They identify the trends seen. There are no simple patterns, but students should describe any general trends.

- Students compare the trends in melting points for periods 4 and 5 given on **worksheet 8.10.2** to those of periods 2 and 3, given on page 165 of the Student book. Again, there are no easy answers – students should describe overall trends, similarities, and differences.

Extension

Use the Internet to find pictures of the elements of periods 2 and 3, and to find out about the uses of the elements of one of these periods. These websites are good places to begin: *rsc.org/periodic-table* and *webelements.com*

Homework

Workbook page 76

Key words

period, trend

CD resources
- Worksheet 8.11.1
- Worksheet 8.11.2

Objective

- Describe how scientists work today

Overview

This enquiry lesson explores the work of scientists looking for the particles that make up protons and electrons, so addressing one of the *Ideas and evidence* statements in the specification. The lesson begins with a brief look at the work of Bose and Einstein in predicting a new state of matter, and the 1964 predictions of Higgs. Students then create a poster about the work of scientists developing and using the Large Hadron Collider to search for the Higgs boson. They gather information for this task either from the Student book, or from the Internet.

Activities

- Students use the Student book to help them complete the flow chart on **worksheet 8.11.1** summarising some of the early work leading to the prediction of the existence of the Higgs boson. They should focus on the processes involved in suggesting explanations, and on how scientists build on each other's ideas.

- Students use information from the Student book, and – optionally – the Internet to create a poster about the Large Hadron Collider. This may include information about its design and the 2012 detection of a new boson. It should emphasise how scientists from many countries are working together on the project, and how electronic communication has made such collaboration possible. **Worksheet 8.11.2** supports this activity.
  Useful websites include:

  - *http://public.web.cern.ch/public/en/lhc-en.html*
  - *www.newscientist.com/topic/larg-hadron-collider*
  - *www.lhc.ac.uk/*

- You can also search for *Large Hadron Collider [country name]* to find out about the contributions of scientists from your country.

Homework

Workbook page 77

Key words

particle, sub-atomic, evidence, explanation, proton

⊘ **CD resource**
- Worksheet 9.1.1

Objective

- Explain the difference between exothermic and endothermic reactions

Overview

This lesson introduces exothermic and endothermic reactions. It begins with a brief demonstration to illustrate an exothermic reaction (burning) and an endothermic change (melting). Through this activity, students are introduced to the terms *exothermic* and *endothermic*. The main part of the lesson is taken up by a practical activity in which students classify four reactions as exothermic or endothermic. They will return to some of these changes in greater detail in future lessons.

Activities

- **Practical activity:** Burn a piece of paper or wood. Through discussion, point out that a chemical reaction is taking place. The reaction releases heat. It is an exothermic change.

  Then place an ice cube on a student's hand. It melts, and the hand feels cold. Tell students that melting ice takes heat from the hand. Melting is an endothermic change.

- **Practical activity:** Students follow the instructions on the **worksheet 9.1.1** to perform four reactions, and classify each change as exothermic or endothermic. Emphasise that, for changes involving solutions:

  - In an exothermic change, the temperature initially increases. This is because the heat released is first used to heat the solution. The heat is then released to the surroundings.

  - In an endothermic change, the temperature initially decreases. This is because the heat needed for the change is taken from the solution, so its temperature decreases. The solution then takes in energy from the surroundings.

Homework

Workbook page 78

Key words

fuel, exothermic, endothermic

CD resources

- Worksheet 9.2.1
- Worksheet 9.2.2

Objective

- Consider how to plan an investigation, obtain evidence, and draw conclusions

Overview

In this lesson, students plan and carry out an investigation to compare the heat released on burning by different fuels. They will plan the investigation themselves. This includes carrying out preliminary work to decide the volume of water to use.

Students then consider their evidence and approach. What is their conclusion? How could they improve their method? What changes could they make to reduce error and improve reliability?

You may need to emphasise that temperature is not the same as heat. The temperature increase of the water is an indication of the heat released by the burning fuel. The greater the temperature increase of the water, the more heat is released by the burning fuel.

Activities

- Introduce students to fuels as materials that burn to release useful heat. Ask students to suggest examples of fuels.

- Display a range of substances that can be used as fuels, for example methanol, ethanol, propan-1-ol, butan-1-ol. Point out that of these fuels, only ethanol is used on a large scale. Students follow the guidance on **worksheet 9.2.1** to plan an investigation to find out which fuel releases most heat on burning. The level of teacher guidance required will depend on students' previous planning experience.

- **Practical activity:** Students follow the guidance on **worksheet 9.2.2** to carry out their investigation, and consider their evidence and approach. Tasks include writing a conclusion, and considering how to reduce error and increase reliability.

Homework

Workbook page 79

Key words

reliable, error, preliminary work

Student book, pages 174–175

CD resource
- Worksheet 9.3.1

Objective

- Consider the advantages and disadvantages of vehicle fuels

Overview

Students begin by listing all the different vehicle fuels they can think of, and outlining their advantages and disadvantages. They then read about three different vehicle fuels. In groups they create, perform, and evaluate a radio or television programme to tell people about these fuels.

Finally, there is an optional activity to research other fuels – perhaps ones that are used locally – and produce a poster about them.

Activities

- In pairs, students list all the different vehicle fuels they can think of, and outline what they know about their advantages and disadvantages.

- Students read pages 174–5 in the Student book about three different vehicle fuels – diesel, hydrogen, and ethanol. In groups of four, they use **worksheet 9.3.1** to help them create a radio or television programme to tell others how these fuels are produced, and about their benefits and disadvantages.

- Student groups perform their programmes to at least one other group. The listening/viewing groups evaluate the programmes according to the criteria at the bottom of **worksheet 9.3.1**.

Extension

Use the Internet to research one or more other fuels – perhaps ones which are used locally – and produce a poster about how they are obtained, and their advantages and disadvantages. A suitable starting point is *www. afdc.energy.gov/fuels/*

Homework

Workbook page 80

Key words

fuels, greenhouse gas, combustion

CD resources
- Worksheet 9.4.1
- Worksheet 9.4.2

Objective

- Describe how to measure the heat released when food burns

Overview

The lesson begins with a discussion about the different amounts of energy provided by different foods. Students then measure the temperature increase of a fixed volume of water caused by burning different foods. They calculate the amount of heat transferred to the water by each food, and compare their results to published energy values for these foods. Student values are likely to be lower than published values, since much heat is transferred to the apparatus and surroundings in their investigation.

Energy from food is covered in more detail in the *Complete Biology for Cambridge Secondary 1* Student book.

Activities

- As a class, discuss foods that provide different amounts of energy. For example, fatty foods provide more energy than green leafy vegetables. Of course, foods with low energy values may still be nutritious.

- Students design and carry out an investigation to compare the heat released on burning different foods. **Worksheet 9.4.1** guides them through the planning process.

- Students follow the guidance on **worksheet 9.4.2** to calculate the amount of energy transferred as heat to the water on burning each food. They use food packets, or the Internet, to find published energy values for these foods. They suggest reasons for differences. The reasons might include the fact that, in the investigation, heat is transferred to the apparatus and surroundings as well as to the water.

Homework

Workbook page 81

Key words

heat, energy, burning

Student book, pages 178–179

⚡ **CD resources**

■ Worksheet 9.5.1

■ Worksheet 9.5.2

Objective

● Plan how to investigate an endothermic process

Overview

The lesson begins with a demonstration to illustrate the cooling that occurs when ammonium nitrate dissolves in water.

Students then plan and carry out an investigation to answer one of three scientific questions about the heat released or taken in when solutes dissolve.

If time allows, students discuss their findings with a group who answered a different investigation question.

Activities

● Demonstrate the process described on page 178 of the Student book in which ammonium nitrate dissolves in water, causing a small amount of water under the flask to freeze. The ice formed sticks the flask to a small block of wood.

● **Practical activity:** Students plan and carry out an investigation to answer one of the three questions below. **Worksheet 9.5.1** supports this activity.

■ For a solute that dissolves endothermically, does the mass of solute affect the amount of heat taken in?
(use from 0.5 g to 3.0 g of ammonium chloride in 10 cm³ of water)

■ For a solute that dissolves endothermically, does the volume of solvent affect the amount of heat taken in?
(use 1.5 g of ammonium chloride in 5–15 cm³ water)

■ Which solutes take in or release the most heat when they dissolve in water?
(solutes listed on activity sheet; use 1 spatula measure of each solid in 25 cm³ water)

● Student groups discuss their results with others who have tackled a different question. They question each other about their planning, and about how they obtained and considered their evidence. **Worksheet 9.5.2** supports this activity.

Homework

Workbook page 82

Key words

endothermic, enquiry, variable, evidence

CD resource
- Worksheet 10.1.1

Objective

- Investigate the burning reactions of metals

Overview

This lesson involves a series of practical activities, in which students try burning metals in air and list the metals in order of the vigour of their reactions.

Students begin by sprinkling iron filings in a Bunsen burner flame. They then burn a piece of magnesium ribbon. They think about their investigation so far – which metal is more reactive? Is the investigation fair? Students then try burning pieces of iron and copper of similar size to the magnesium ribbon to more fairly compare the vigour of their reactions.

Finally, students compare the reaction of aluminium and oxygen with that of iron and oxygen.

Activities

- **Practical activity:** Students sprinkle a spatula measure of iron filings into a hot Bunsen flame, and record their observations. **Worksheet 10.1.1** supports this activity.

- **Practical activity (continued):** Students burn magnesium ribbon in a Bunsen flame, and record their observations. Students should not look directly at the magnesium as it burns, since the bright white flame can cause eye damage. **Worksheet 10.1.1** supports this activity.

- **Practical activity (continued):** Ask students to compare the vigour of reaction of iron and magnesium with oxygen from the air. Guide students to the conclusion that it is not fair to compare the two burning reactions, since the metal pieces are of different sizes. Give students pieces of iron and copper of similar size to the magnesium ribbon. Ask them to compare the vigour of the reactions of the three metals when heated in air. **Worksheet 10.1.1** supports this activity.

- Students write equations for the reactions they have observed. Questions 2 and 3 on **worksheet 10.1.1** sheet support this activity.

Extension

Demonstrate the burning reaction of aluminium powder by sprinkling it into a Bunsen flame. Compare the vigour of the reaction with that of iron.

Homework

Workbook page 83

Key words

preliminary work, burning, metals, oxygen, oxide

Student book, pages 184–185

Objective

- Describe how metals react with water

Overview

This lesson starts with a look at metals that do not react with water, and why they are useful. Students then try reacting five metals with water. They note the vigour of the reactions and test the gaseous product formed. Students then observe as the teacher demonstrates the reaction of lithium with water. The lesson concludes with a comparison of the reactions of metals with oxygen (see lesson 10.1) and with water. Do metals that react vigorously with oxygen also react vigorously with water?

Activities

- Students look at the cartoon at the top of page 184 of the Student book. They discuss these questions: Why is it useful that some metals do not react with water? Which metals do not react with water?

- **Practical activity:** Students add five metals to water – copper, magnesium, calcium, lead, and iron. They observe and compare the vigour of their reactions with water. **Worksheet 10.2.1** supports this activity.

- **Practical activity (continued):** Students repeat the test with calcium, this time testing the gas produced to find out if it is hydrogen or oxygen. The gas is hydrogen. There is a pattern in the reactions – all metals that react with water produce hydrogen gas. Students write equations for the reactions they have observed. **Worksheet 10.2.1** supports this activity.

- Demonstrate the reaction of lithium with water. Test to show that the gas produced is hydrogen. Part 1 of **worksheet 10.2.2** supports this activity. *Lesson 8.6 includes a similar demonstration.*

- Students list the metals tested in order of reactivity. In pairs, they discuss whether metals that react vigorously with oxygen also react vigorously with water. Part 2 of **worksheet 10.2.2** supports this activity.

Homework

Workbook page 84

Key words

reaction, metal, water, hydroxide

CD resources

- Worksheet 10.3.1
- Worksheet 10.3.2

Objective

- Describe how metals react with acids

Overview

Students begin by predicting whether copper or magnesium will react more vigorously with acid. They then plan an investigation to compare the vigour of the reactions of five metals with hydrochloric acid. Students then carry out their investigation, and compare the pattern observed to those of the metals with oxygen and water. As an extension task, students write word equations for the reactions observed, and predict the products of the reactions of metals with other acids.

Activities

- Students discuss which is likely to react with hydrochloric acid more vigorously – copper or magnesium, and justify their choice.
- Students plan an investigation to compare the vigour of the reactions of magnesium, lead, iron, zinc, and copper with hydrochloric acid. **Worksheet 10.3.1** guides them to consider how to make the test fair, how to manage risk, and how to test the gaseous product.
- Students carry out their investigation, and list the metals used in order of the vigour of their reactions with hydrochloric acid. They compare this pattern with those of the metals with oxygen and water. Part 1 and questions 1 and 2 on **worksheet 10.3.2** support this activity.

Extension

Students write word equations for the reactions observed, and for the reactions of metals with sulfuric acid. Questions 3 and 4 on **worksheet 10.3.2** support this activity.

Homework

Workbook page 85

Key words

acids, metal, hazard, risk, hydrogen

Student book, pages 188–189

⚙ **CD resources**

- Worksheet 10.4.1
- Worksheet 10.4.2

Objective

- Understand the reactivity series

Overview

Students begin by considering their findings from lessons 10.1, 10.2, and 10.3, and organise metal information cards in order of reactivity. They then write down the reactivity series, and make some notes about it.

Students then look at links between the reactivity series and corrosion. They predict which metals will corrode most and least easily, and then make a poster describing and explaining different techniques of preventing corrosion.

Activities

- Student groups study the metal reaction data on the cards on **worksheet 10.4.1**, and place the cards in order of metal reactivity.

- Students list metals in order of reactivity, and read pages 188–9 of the Student book to note key points about the reactivity series.

- Students use the reactivity series to predict which metal will corrode most easily. Question 1 of **worksheet 10.4.2** supports this activity.

- Students make a poster describing and explaining different techniques of preventing corrosion. Question 2 of **worksheet 10.4.2** supports this activity.

Extension

Students use the Internet to do further research about preventing corrosion of metal objects at sea, for example offshore wind farms, oil rigs, and ships. Start by searching for *corrosion prevention oil rig*.

Homework

Workbook page 86

Key words

corrosion, reactivity series

⚫ **CD resource**
■ Worksheet 10.5.1

Objective

- Plan an enquiry and interpret evidence to work out the position of an unknown metal in the reactivity series

Overview

This lesson is about the position of metals in the reactivity series. The lesson starts with a quick introduction to nickel. Students then interpret secondary evidence, and plan how they would collect and interpret primary evidence. The secondary data given on the worksheet is for nickel; but nickel and its salts are toxic only allow students to plan their investigations. Do not carry them out in the classroom.

Activities

- Introduce the lesson with a review of the reactivity series. Students should recall what they have learnt in lesson 10.4.
- Tell students they will plan an investigation to find the position of a metal in the reactivity series. Ask pairs to discuss how to approach this task.
- Students examine secondary data about the burning reactions of metal powders. They use secondary data to compare the reactions of an unknown metal and other metals with dilute hydrochloric acid, and interpret the data collected. **Worksheet 10.5.1** supports this activity.

Extension

Tell the students that the unknown metal is nickel. Students then use the Internet to find out more about nickel. How are its properties linked to its uses? Start by looking at these websites: *rsc.org/periodic-table* and *webelements.com*

Homework

Workbook page 87

Key words

reactivity series, nickel, corrosion, evidence

Student book, pages 192–193

CD resources
- Worksheet 10.6.1
- Worksheet 10.6.2

Objective

- Explain what displacement reactions are, and how they are useful

Overview

This lesson begins by looking at copper – why is it useful? How is it extracted from copper ore waste? Students carry out reactions in which more reactive metals displace less reactive metals from their compounds. The lesson concludes with a demonstration of the dramatic thermite reaction, in which aluminium displaces iron from one of its oxides.

Activities

- Introduce copper as a vital metal, useful for electric cables and water pipes. Copper ore supplies are running out, so companies extract copper from copper ore waste. Students read about how this is done on page 192 of the Student book. Set up a demonstration by immersing an iron nail in copper sulfate solution. Return to this towards the end of the lesson to observe the copper formed.

- **Practical activity:** Tell students the reaction of iron with copper sulfate solution is a displacement reaction. In these reactions, a more reactive metal displaces a less reactive metal from its compounds. Students predict which metal – salt solution pairs react, and carry out a practical to test their predications. **Worksheet 10.6.1** supports this activity.

- Demonstrate the thermite reaction. This is described in detail at *www.nuffieldfoundation.org/practical-chemistry/thermite-reaction*. It is vital to follow the safety guidance. Students then tackle questions about this reaction on **worksheet 10.6.2**.

- Watch a video clip in which the thermite reaction is used to weld railway rails together. Search online for *thermite welding railway* to find a video clip.

Extension

Demonstrate the burning reaction of aluminium powder by sprinkling it into a Bunsen flame. Compare the vigour of the reaction with that of iron.

Homework

Workbook page 88

Key words

displaced, displacement reaction, thermite reaction

CD resources
- Worksheet 10.7.1
- Worksheet 10.7.2

Objective

- Explain the link between the position of a metal in the reactivity series, and how the metal is extracted from its ore.

Overview

This lesson links the reactivity series with metal extraction techniques. First, students consider gold. They use panning to separate the metal (or something that looks like it!) from a mixture of sand and water. Students then use carbon to extract copper and iron from their oxides. Finally, they learn that electrolysis is used to extract metals that are high in the reactivity series.

Activities

- **Practical activity:** Introduce gold as an unreactive metal at the bottom of the reactivity series. Since it is unreactive, it is found as an element in the Earth's crust. In some areas, gold is found in stream beds, mixed with sand and gravel. Students use panning to separate iron pyrites – or another substance that looks like gold, and has a high density – from a mixture of sand and water. **Worksheet 10.7.1** supports this activity.

- **Practical activity:** Iron and copper are towards the middle of the reactivity series. They are extracted from their naturally-occurring compounds by heating with carbon. Students heat the two metal oxides with carbon powder to illustrate this process. **Worksheet 10.7.2** supports this activity.

- Tell students that aluminium and metals above it in the reactivity series are strongly joined to other elements in compounds. These metals cannot be extracted from their compounds by heating with carbon. Instead, they are extracted by electrolysis. Students find out more about this process by reading page 195 of the Student book and by watching a video clip. Search online for *aluminium extraction – Royal Society of Chemistry* for a video clip.

Homework

Workbook page 89

Key words

ore, metal, extracting metals, reactivity

CD resources
- Worksheet 10.8.1
- Worksheet 10.8.2
- Worksheet 10.8.3

Objective

- Write balanced symbol equations for simple reactions.

Overview

This lesson begins with a quick look at word equations, and why they are useful. Students are then guided through the process of interpreting symbol equations. Next, students use displayed formula cards to help them balance symbol equations for burning and displacement reactions. The lesson concludes with a chance to balance unbalanced symbol equations and write balanced symbol equations given word equations and formulae.

Activities

- Through discussion, elicit that word equations are useful because they show the reactants and products in a reaction. Students practise writing word equations on Part 1 of **worksheet 10.8.1**.

- Explain that symbol equations give more information about a reaction. They give formulae, relative amounts, and show how atoms are rearranged. Students learn how to interpret symbol equations using Part 2 of **worksheet 10.8.1**.

- Students use displayed formula as a first stage in helping them to balance equations. **Worksheet 10.8.2** supports this activity.

- Go through the stages given on pages 196–7 of the Student book to show students how to balance equations for burning magnesium and burning lithium. Students then balance unbalanced symbol equations and write balanced symbol equations given word equations and formulae on **worksheet 10.8.3**.

Homework

Workbook page 90

Key words

chemical symbol, burning, state symbols, equations

CD resources
- Worksheet 11.1.1
- Worksheet 11.1.2

Objective

- Describe how to make salts by reacting acids with metals

Overview

The lesson starts with a look at salts – can students remember what they are? They then make their own salt – magnesium chloride – by reacting magnesium with dilute hydrochloric acid. Before the practical, students make choices about the best equipment to use. The lesson ends with questions about the different stages of the practical, focusing on the purpose of each stage.

Activities

- Display crystals of different salts. Include coloured salts, for example copper sulfate and salts of iron. Remind students that a salt is a compound made when a metal replaces hydrogen in an acid.

- Tell students they will make their own salt. Display apparatus pairs, as below, and ask students to choose the more suitable piece of apparatus from each pair.
  - Measuring cylinder or beaker to measure acid volume.
  - Filter paper and funnel or sieve to separate solid magnesium from magnesium chloride solution.

- **Practical activity:** Students follow the instructions to make magnesium chloride crystals from magnesium and dilute hydrochloric acid. **Worksheet 11.1.1** supports this activity.

- Students answer the questions on **worksheet 11.1.2** about the purpose of each stage of the practical, and about making other salts.

Homework

Workbook page 91

Key words

salt, compound, acid, metal

Student book, pages 202–203

CD resources

- Worksheet 11.2.1
- Worksheet 11.2.2

Objective

- Describe how to make salts by reacting acids with carbonates

Overview

The lesson starts with a look at copper sulfate. How is it useful? Having assessed hazards, students make copper sulfate from copper carbonate and sulfuric acid. They consider how to maximise the yield of the product, and write word equations to summarise the reactions of other carbonates with acids.

Activities

- Display crystals of copper sulfate. Ask how the salt is useful. One use is as a fungicide – farmers use it to control fungi on grape plants.

- Tell students they will make their own copper sulfate crystals. Ask students to identify hazards, and suggest how to minimise risk from these hazards. Use **worksheet 11.2.1** as teacher support only at this stage.

- **Practical activity:** Students follow instructions to make copper sulfate crystals from copper carbonate and dilute sulfuric acid. **Worksheet 11.2.1** supports this activity.

- Students answer questions about the procedure they have followed, particularly about maximising the yield of the product, and write word equations for other carbonate – acid reactions. **Worksheet 11.2.2** supports this activity.

Homework

Workbook page 92

Key words

equation, salt, compound, acid, carbonate

CD resources

- Worksheet 11.3.1
- Worksheet 11.3.2

Objective

- Describe how to make salts by reacting acids with alkalis

Overview

The lesson starts with a look at sodium chloride. What is it used for? Why is it extracted from the sea, or mined from rock, rather than made in the laboratory? Students then prepare samples of sodium chloride by reacting hydrochloric acid with sodium carbonate. Two methods are given, so that half the class can follow each method. Having prepared their salt, students compare the two methods. Which gives a greater amount of product from given amounts of starting materials? Why?

Activities

- Display sodium chloride. Elicit that it is used to flavour and preserve food, and to make other chemicals such as chlorine and sodium hydroxide. Explain that sodium chloride is extracted from sea or mined from rock. It is not made in the laboratory since the process would be very expensive and is unnecessary since large amounts of the substance exist naturally.

- Tell students they will make their own sodium chloride by neutralising dilute hydrochloric acid with sodium carbonate solution. They cannot use the same method as in lessons 11.1 or 11.2 since both reactants are soluble. Students will follow one of two methods as shown on **worksheets 11.3.1** and **11.3.2**. Students may need guidance using the pipette and burette in method 2.

- Students compare the two methods. Which gives a greater amount of product from given amounts of starting materials? Why? The answer is that the titration method produces less product since this method involves discarding the first sample of sodium chloride solution that is made. Student book page 205 can be used to guide the discussion.

Homework

Workbook page 93

Key words

salt, acid, alkali, neutralise

CD resource
- Worksheet 11.4.1

Objective

- Identify salts used as fertilisers

Overview

The lesson begins with a discussion about fertilisers. Why do farmers add them to crops? Which salts do plants require? Students then make a soluble salt – ammonium sulfate – that is used as a fertiliser. If time allows, they use information from the Student book and/or the Internet to create a poster to show why plants need nitrogen, phosphorus, and potassium minerals.

Activities

- Ask students why farmers add fertilisers to crops. Elicit that they may use natural fertilisers, such as manure and compost, and synthetic fertilisers, such as ammonium compounds.

- **Practical activity:** Students follow the instructions on **worksheet 11.4.1** to make a fertiliser salt, ammonium sulfate. The salt is soluble in water, and so are the compounds it is made from. This means that it is not possible to filter off an excess of one reactant. Instead, students will detect the end of the reaction by smelling when ammonia is present in excess, and by then removing a small sample and checking it is alkaline.

- Students use information from pages 206–207 of the Student book, or the Internet, to create a poster to show why plants need nitrogen, phosphorus, and potassium minerals.

Homework

Workbook page 94

Key words

salt, fertiliser, plants, ammonia, nitrogen, phosphorous, potassium

CD resources
- Worksheet 12.1.1
- Worksheet 12.1.2

Objective

- Understand how to follow the rate of reaction that produces a gas

Overview

This lesson introduces rates of reaction. The first activity asks students to consider why reaction rate is important, and to give examples of slow and fast reactions. The main activity of the lesson is a practical, in which students follow the reaction of dilute hydrochloric acid with magnesium. Students then plot graphs to show the progress of the reaction, and finish by interpreting these.

Activities

- Student pairs give examples of fast and slow reactions, and consider why chemists might want to change the rate of a reaction. Read page 210 of the Student book.

- **Practical activity:** Students follow the reaction of dilute hydrochloric acid with magnesium by measuring the volume of hydrogen gas made every 10 seconds. They record their results in a table. **Worksheet 12.1.1** supports this activity.

- Students use the guidance on **worksheet 12.1.2** to plot a line graph of gas volume against time. They then answer questions to help them interpret the graph – they are likely to need help with this task. The graph shows that the reaction is fastest at the beginning. The rate gradually falls as the magnesium is used up. The reaction finishes when all the magnesium is used up. This is shown by the horizontal section of the graph.

Homework

Workbook page 95

Key words

reaction rate, patterns, collisions

⚙ **CD resources**

- Worksheet 12.2.1
- Worksheet 12.2.2
- Worksheet 12.2.3

Objective

- Describe and explain how concentration affects reaction rate

Overview

In this lesson students consider factors that affect reaction rates. They then investigate one of these factors, the concentration of solution. The reaction chosen is the same as that in lesson 12.1, so as to make it possible for students to devise their own investigation. Having planned and carried out their investigation, students draw a graph and write a conclusion. They then consider the approach and note down suggestions for reducing error and obtaining more reliable results. Finally, student use a model to explain why increasing concentration increases rate.

Activities

- Lead a discussion to elicit factors that may have changed the rate of the reaction studied in lesson 12.1. Students might suggest acid concentration, temperature, or size of magnesium pieces. Adding a catalyst might also change its rate, although students are unlikely to suggest this.

- Students follow the guidance on **worksheet 12.2.1** to design an investigation to study the effect of concentration on reaction rate. They then carry out their investigations.

- Students use their data to plot a line graph and write a conclusion for their investigation. The higher the acid concentration, the faster the reaction. Students consider how to reduce error and obtain more reliable results. They could do this by repeating the investigation three times at each concentration, and calculating the mean. **Worksheet 12.2.2** supports this activity.

- **Practical activity:** Pairs use uncooked rice and beans, and pieces of cardboard, to model the reaction and to help them explain why increasing concentration increases rate. **Worksheet 12.2.3** supports this activity.

Homework

Workbook page 96

Key words

reaction rate, concentration, correlation, evidence

Student book, pages 214–215

CD resources
- Worksheet 12.3.1
- Worksheet 12.3.2

Objective

- Describe and explain how temperature affects reaction rate

Overview

In this lesson students investigate the effect of temperature on the rate of the reaction of sodium thiosulfate with hydrochloric acid. Having obtained, presented and considered their evidence, extension students suggest how they could investigate the effect of temperature on the rate of another reaction. The lesson finishes with modelling an explanation for the findings of the lesson – at higher temperatures, particles move faster. This makes them collide more frequently, and increases the number of successful collisions in a given time.

Activities

- Ask students whether potatoes/cassava cook faster in boiling oil or in boiling water. Elicit that the reason for quicker cooking in boiling oil is that its temperature is higher.
- **Practical activity:** Students carry out an investigation to study the effect of temperature on reaction rate. Students must work in a well-ventilated room, and wear eye protection. **Worksheet 12.3.1** supports this activity.
- Students use their data to plot a line graph to display their results. Part 1 of **worksheet 12.3.2** supports this activity.
- Students make a human model to explain the findings of the lesson. Half the students take roles of particles from sodium thiosulfate solution, the other students are particles from hydrochloric acid. Students move around. At 'low temperatures' they move slowly. Their collisions are infrequent. At 'higher temperatures' they move faster. Their collisions are more frequent. The reaction is faster. Read page 215 of the Student book.
- Students complete Part 2 of **worksheet 12.3.2**.

Extension

Students plan how to investigate the effect of temperature on the reaction rate of hydrochloric acid and magnesium. They do not carry out this practical.

Homework

Workbook page 97

Key words

reaction rate, temperature

Student book, pages 216–217

CD resource
- Worksheet 12.4.1

Objective

- Describe and explain how surface area affects reaction rate

Overview

This lesson shows how surface area affects reaction rate. It starts with a dramatic demonstration, either in the lab or as a video clip. Students then watch a demonstration of the effect of increasing surface area on the rate of reaction of calcium carbonate with dilute hydrochloric acid. They record the results and draw a bar chart. Finally, students draw diagrams to explain the results using ideas about colliding particles.

Activities

- Use a Bunsen burner to try to set fire to a small pile of cornflour (very fine maize flour). Then show the impact of increasing surface area – either as a video clip (search YouTube for *flour explosion the Barton special*) or by performing the demonstration shown on the video clip yourself.
- Demonstrate the effect of increasing surface area on the rate of the reaction of calcium carbonate with dilute hydrochloric acid, following the procedure on **worksheet 12.4.1**. This can be tackled as a class practical if you have enough balances.
- Students follow the guidance on **worksheet 12.4.1**, and use information from pages 216–7 of the Student book, to write a conclusion for the investigation. This should include diagrams to explain the results using ideas about colliding particles.

Extension

Students devise an investigation to find out about the effect of increasing surface area on the reaction of hydrochloric acid with magnesium.

Homework

Workbook page 98

Key words

reaction rate, surface area, predictions, evidence

Student book, pages 218–219

CD resources

- Worksheet 12.5.1
- Worksheet 12.5.2

Objective

- Describe and explain how catalysts affects reaction rate

Overview

The lesson begins with a review of learning so far – what factors affect reaction rate? There is then a short demonstration to show students the effect of adding liver to hydrogen peroxide. Students then investigate the effectiveness of other catalysts in speeding up the decomposition of hydrogen peroxide solution, and draw a bar chart to display their results. The lesson ends with a research task on catalysts, and the creation of posters to display findings.

Activities

- Briefly review learning on reaction rates by asking students what factors affect reaction rate. Tell students that they will now investigate one final factor – catalysts. Demonstrate adding a small piece of sheep or chicken liver to 2.5 vol hydrogen peroxide solution. Bubbles of oxygen gas, which relight a glowing splint, are produced. By the end of the lesson students should be able to explain their observations.

- **Practical activity:** Students investigate the effectiveness of different catalysts in speeding up the decomposition of hydrogen peroxide solution. **Worksheet 12.5.1** supports this activity. They present their results on bar charts. Parts 1 and 2 of **worksheet 12.5.2** support this activity.

- Go back to the liver demonstration. Elicit an explanation for the observations – a substance in liver (catalase) has speeded up the decomposition reaction of hydrogen peroxide. Explain that catalase is an enzyme. Enzymes are a type of natural catalyst found in most cells.

- Students research uses for catalysts, and make posters to display their findings. Part 3 of **worksheet 12.5.2** supports this activity.

Homework

Workbook page 99

Key words

catalyst, enzyme, reaction rate

1 States of matter

1.1 The particle theory of matter

1

	solid	liquid	gas
How close are the particles?	Touching	Touching	Not touching
Are the particles in a pattern?	Regular pattern	No regular pattern	No regular pattern
How do the particles move?	Particles don't move – they vibrate on the spot	Particles move around, in and out of each other	Particles move very fast in all directions
How strongly do the particles attract each other?	Strongly attracted	Strongly attracted	Very weakly attracted

2 When you press a solid metal hard, the shape does not change because the particles are already touching so they cannot get closer together.

3 In the solid and liquid states the particles are touching and cannot get any closer. In the gas state, the particles are not touching so they can be compressed (squashed together).

1.2 Boiling, evaporating, and condensing

1 condensation

2 The particles move faster and spread out.

3 nitrogen

4 Heat the metal using an electric heater. When the temperature stops rising, the scientist has found the boiling point.

1.3 Questions, evidence, and explanations

1 Collect data for the boiling points of other liquids (e.g. ethanol) at different altitudes.

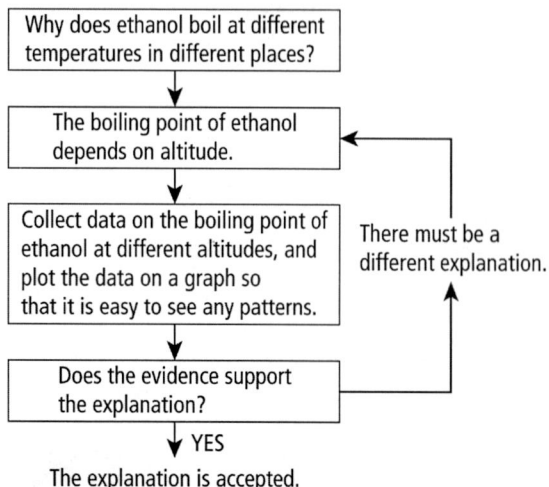

```
┌─────────────────────────────────┐
│ Why does ethanol boil at different│
│ temperatures in different places? │
└─────────────────────────────────┘
              ↓
┌─────────────────────────────────┐
│ The boiling point of ethanol     │ ←────┐
│ depends on altitude.             │      │
└─────────────────────────────────┘      │
              ↓                           │
┌─────────────────────────────────┐  ┌──────────────┐
│ Collect data on the boiling point│  │ There must be a│
│ of ethanol at different altitudes,│  │ different      │
│ and plot the data on a graph so  │  │ explanation.   │
│ that it is easy to see any       │  └──────────────┘
│ patterns.                        │      ↑
└─────────────────────────────────┘      │
              ↓                           │
┌─────────────────────────────────┐      │
│ Does the evidence support        │ ─────┘
│ the explanation?                 │
└─────────────────────────────────┘
              ↓ YES
   The explanation is accepted.
```

2 Given the new evidence, Rabia can now consider her previous knowledge about what boiling is. Rabia can conclude that at a higher altitude, for a given volume, less energy (heat) is required to reach boiling point.

1.4 Melting, freezing, and subliming

1 melting

2 Particles stop moving around, arrange themselves in a regular pattern and vibrate on the spot.

3 Jati could heat the sample until it melts whilst measuring the temperature. If the substance melts at the same temperature it is pure. If the substance melts over a range of temperatures it is a mixture.

1.5 Energy and changes of state

1 The forces between the particles get weaker when a liquid becomes a gas.

2 When particles evaporate, some of the faster-moving particles have enough energy to overcome the forces holding the particles together and they can break free from the surface of the liquid.

3 Gold. Substances with higher boiling points have stronger forces between the particles and require more energy to separate the particles.

1.6 Using particle theory to explain dissolving

1 **Dissolve:** When the particles of a solid randomly mix with the particles of a liquid to form a random arrangement.
Solution: A mixture of solute dissolved in a solvent.
Solvent: A liquid in which a solute can dissolve.
Solute: A substance that can dissolve in a solvent.
Solubility: The mass of a substance that can dissolve in 100 g of water.

2 Find the mass of the water and the container. Find the mass of the salt. Dissolve the salt in the water. Find the mass of the solution. The mass should be the total of the water, salt, and container.

3 Add 1 g of salt to 100 g of water and mix until dissolved. Repeat until the salt will not dissolve. Repeat the experiment to check the result.

4 **a** Lithium chloride
b Sodium chloride
c Approximately 73–4 grams per 100g of water.

1.7 Planning an investigation

1 A variable is a quality or characteristic that can change.

2 To ensure that her investigation is a fair test.

3 Zahra could add 5 g of salt to 100 cm³ and stir at different speeds e.g. 1 rotation per second, timing how long it takes for the salt to dissolve.
Variables: speed of stirring, water temperature, water volume, mass of salt, size of salt grains.
Variable to change: speed of stirring.
Variable to observe: time for salt to dissolve.

Apparatus: measuring cylinder, beaker, laboratory thermometer, electronic balance (for accuracy) OR balance with weights (reliability of electricity), stirring rod, stopwatch.

1.8 Presenting evidence

1 A variable whose values are words or certain numerical values.
2 To look for patterns in her results.
3 Continuous data is best shown on a line graph.
4 A bar chart as the variable he is changing (the substance) is discrete.

1.9 Review

1a Particles do not move around, but vibrate whilst touching each other.
  b In ice the particles are arranged in a regular pattern, in water the particles are arranged randomly.
2a C
  b D
  c melting
3a In gases, the particles do not touch each other, they move around very quickly and there are weak forces of attraction between the particles.
  b As the particles in gases are not touching they can be compressed (pushed closer together).
4 The particles get further apart.
5a increases
  b decreases
  c decreases
6 Top to bottom: C, B, and A
7a krypton
  b krypton
  c chlorine and krypton
  d iodine and osmium
  e liquid, gas
  f boiling
8a liquid
  b melting
9a C
  b A
10a time
  b temperature
  c

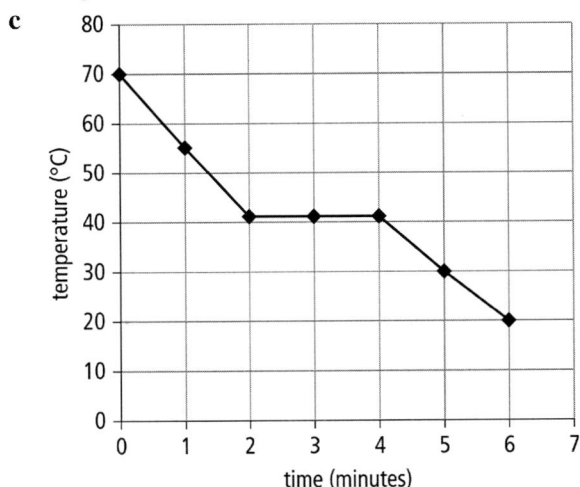

d freezing point = 42 °C
e Particles slow down, move less, and arrange themselves into a regular pattern and vibrate in the same place.
11a i temperature of water
  ii mass of potassium chloride that dissolves
  iii volume of water
     amount of stirring
  b Yes, the graph shows that as the temperature increases, the mass of potassium chloride that dissolves increases.

12a

Substance tested	Mass of substance that dissolved in 100 g of water (g)
Sodium chloride	36
Potassium chloride	34
Potassium nitrate	47

b

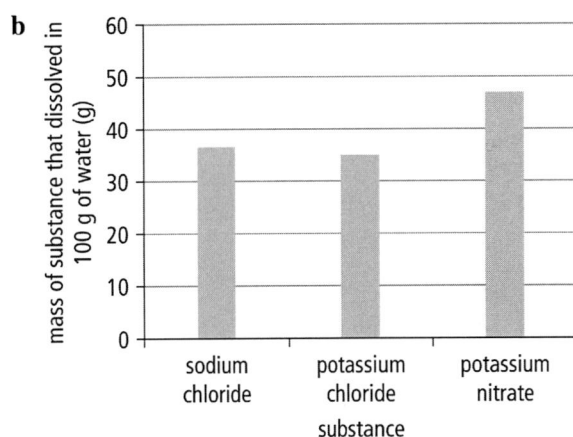

c The variable that is being changed (substance tested) is discrete.
d (electric or weighted) balance, thermometer, beaker, stirring rod,

2 Material properties

2.1 Introducing elements

1 A substance that cannot be split into anything simpler.
2 Metals and non metals
3 **Metals:** any elements to the left of the red line. **Non-metals:** any elements to the right of the red line. Hydrogen is also a non-metal.
4 Any two of the following: conduct electricity, solid at room temperature, shiny, conduct heat, strong, hard, heavy, malleable, ductile.

2.2 Metal elements

1 High melting and boiling points, shiny, sonorous, conductors of heat and electricity, strong, hard, dense (high density), malleable, ductile.
2 Shiny, strong, malleable, ductile.
3 Strong, malleable, hard.

2.3 Non-metal elements

1 Low boiling and melting points, not shiny (dull), brittle, cannot conduct electricity.

2 Dull, brittle, and cannot conduct electricity.

3

Diamond	Graphite
Particles arranged in crystals	Particles arranged in layers
Hard	Soft
Does not conduct electricity	Conducts electricity

2.4 Making conclusions from data

1 iron

2 X, non-metal: not shiny, does not conduct electricity, low melting and boiling points.

Y, EITHER metal: shiny and silver, conducts electricity OR non-metal: low melting and boiling points.

Z, metal: shiny and silver, conducts electricity and has high melting and boiling points.

3 As the force applied increases, the extension of the spring increases.

4 Most metals have melting points above 1000 °C. Lithium and sodium (both Group 1 metals) have melting points of below 200 °C.

2.5 Metal alloys

1 A mixture of metals.

2 The composition of pure aluminium is 100% aluminium. Aluminium alloy 7075 contains 90% aluminium. Pure aluminium has a lower density, is less hard, and is weaker than the aluminium alloy 7075.

3 Low carbon steel is used to build bridges, buildings, and objects that need to be strong. Low carbon steel is strong and easily shaped (malleable).

Manganese steel is used for mining equipment and railway points. It needs to be strong, hard, and be used with large forces. Manganese steel is hard and tough.

Stainless steel is used for knives and forks, and surgical instruments. It need to be able to be used and washed several times. Stainless steel does not rust.

4 See the "particles in iron" and "particles in steel" diagrams (page 35). The particles in iron are arranged in layers and the particles can slide over each other easily making iron soft and weak. In steel, the particles of the other elements are mixed with the iron particles. This mixture stops the iron particles from being able to slide over each other in layers, making steel harder and stronger than pure iron.

2.6 Material properties

1 Cotton is soft, flexible, and allows air through small holes making it comfortable to wear.

2 Sisal is used to make rope because it is strong when pulled.

3 Flexible, strong, waterproof, tough.

2.7 Polmers

1 Polymers are substances that have very long particles.

2 Any six from: poly(ethene), poly(propene), poly(chloroethene) / poly(vinyl chloride)/(PVC), cotton, silk, wool, wood.

3 It is difficult to break up the particles.

4 PVC is used for underground water pipes, insulation on electric cables, and for waterproof clothes. PVC is waterproof and flexible which makes it suitable for bending and covering objects whilst keeping them dry (or keeping water in).

2.8 Review

1a It melts at 1063 °C.

b It is good conductor of electricity. It is a good conductor of heat.

c It melts at 1063 °C (to make it harder to make forgeries) and/or it is always shiny.

d It melts at 1063 °C. It is good conductor of electricity.

2a C

b A: is green, does not conduct electricity, and has a low melting point.

D: is dull yellow, does not conduct electricity, and has a low melting point.

3a a good conductor of heat

b a good conductor of electricity

c sonorous

d strong

4a Substance and weights added.

b Length of wire, same equipment used, e.g. same hangers, weights, clamp stand, etc.

c i copper

ii

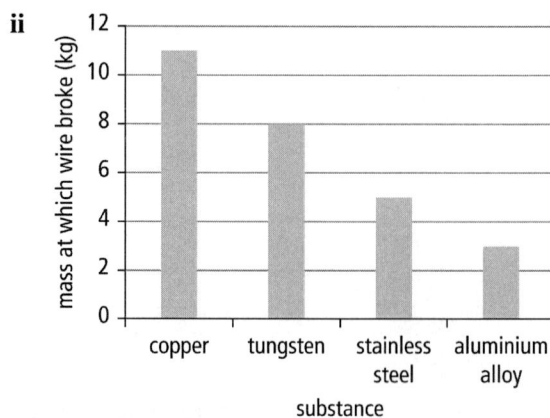

5a waterproof, transparent

b waterproof, flexible

c waterproof, flexible, and strong

d waterproof, strong

e absorbent

6a Poly(propene) does not rot and is stronger than manila fibre.

b Manila is obtained from a plant whereas poly(propene) is made from oil, which is harder to get.

c i 54–55 kN

ii 35–36 mm

iii As the diameter of the manila rope increases, the breaking strength increases at an increasing rate.

iv 30 mm manila rope

7a wood

b concrete

c Wood conducts heat the least, so a house would heat up less in the sun, keeping it cool inside.

d Limestone is stronger than wood.

8a The data (about the substance) is discrete and is best compared in a bar chart.

b Tin, magnesium & platinum, zinc, aluminium, gold, copper.

3 Material changes

3.1 Acids and alkalis

1 Hydrochloric acid, ascorbic acid, omega-3 fatty acids, ethanoic acid (vinegar), methanoic acid, sulfuric acid, nitric acid.

2 Sodium hydroxide is extremely corrosive, it can cause skin to blister, or blind someone if it gets into their eyes. Use eye protection and make sure not to get it on your skin.

3 Acids taste sour. Alkalis feel soapy.

a Oceania

b 53%

3.2 The pH scale and indicators

1 Acidic: red. Alkali: blue or purple.

2 alkaline

3 pH 4 is more acidic

4 A white bowl or plate, a glass with white paper behind. An observer can view the colour clearly if the solution is placed in front of a white background.

3.3 Neutralisation

1 Neutralisation is the cancelling out of an acid by an alkali, or of an alkali by an acid.

2 acid

3 acid

3.4 Planning investigations and collecting evidence

1 Kali keeps the variables the same to ensure a fair test.

2 Measuring cylinders measure smaller differences than beakers (they are more accurate).

3 More logical, scientific, clear, less vague than others.

3.5 Review

1 less than, more than, equal to

2a Top to bottom: acidic, acidic, acidic, alkaline

b Indigestion medicine.

c Sweat, cola drink, or orange juice.

3a Top: red, bottom: blue.

b Red at start, (green at 100 cm³) blue at end.

4a The extra acid comes out in urine, lowering the pH.

b The pH of the urine increases as extra alkali comes out in the urine.

c There would be more alkali in her urine, increasing the pH of her urine and lowering the pH of her blood.

5a cassava

b pineapple and cassava

c The farmer could try growing any of the crops.

d i maize and cassava

ii Acid to lower the soil pH.

6a beaker

b funnel and conical flask

c test tube

7a 6.0

b The acidity increased.

c Trout, salmon, eel, frog, snail, mayfly.

d frog

e The pH must have increased.

f i Mayflies cannot live in pH 5.0.

ii Yes, the pH had increased to 6.0 which mayflies can live in.

8a Measuring cylinders are more accurate as they can measure smaller amounts.

b Top to bottom: concentration of alkali, volume of acid, concentration of acid, volume of alkali, type of indicator.

c i–iii

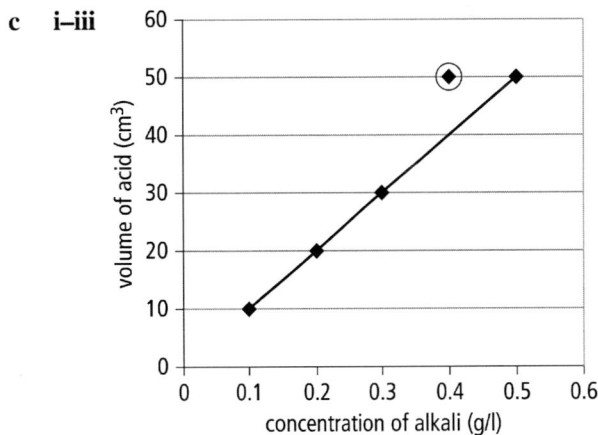

4 The Earth

4.1 The structure of the Earth

1 Inner core, outer core, mantle, crust.

2 Ships sink as they go over the horizon. Aristotle's observations of the Earth's shadow on the Moon.

3 Shockwave patterns produced by earthquakes support the theory that the Earth has a solid inner core.

4.2 Igneous rocks

1. Hard, durable, non-porous.
2. Substances that exist naturally as crystals.
3. Granite is a mixture of minerals that are different colours.
4. Basalt cools quicker than granite, so the crystals have less time to form.

4.3 Sedimentary rocks

1. Sandstone, claystone, mudstone, limestone.
2. Claystone has tiny grains and it is easy to mould wet clay into different shapes.
   Sandstone is a hard sedimentary rock making it a good building material.
3. Use a hand lens and water:
   Look at it with a hand lens – she could see separate grains with spaces between them. If she puts water on the rock, it will absorb the water. If she submerges it in a beaker, bubbles will appear from the air inside the rock. If it is a sedimentary rock she will be able to scratch it.
4. Porous – due to small spaces between the grains within the rock.
   Soft (relative to igneous) as the grains are held together less strongly than the crystals in igneous rocks.

4.4 Sedimentary rock formation

1. Water: pebbles can be transported along a river bed.
   Wind: grains of sand can be transported.
   Gravity: rocks and sediment can be moved by rock falls and landslides.
2. Weathering is the breakdown of rock into sediments.
3. Physical weathering: freeze-thaw weathering from water freezing in cracks, expanding and (after many repetitions) causing the rock to break.

   Chemical weathering: acidic rain falling onto rocks can create new substances.

   Biological weathering: tree roots can grow into rock cracks, slowly breaking the rock. Lichens make chemicals that break down rock.

4.5 Metamorphic rocks

1. Marble, slate, gneiss.
2. Metamorphic rocks are formed when rocks are changed by high temperatures or pressures.
3. Metamorphic rocks have interlocking crystals with no air spaces, so they cannot absorb water.
4. Use a hand lens – sedimentary rocks have separate grains, metamorphic rocks have crystals. Drop some water onto the rock – sedimentary rocks will absorb it, metamorphic rocks will not.

4.6 Questions, evidence, and explanations: the rock cycle

1. Scientists ask a question, make observations and collect evidence, describe the evidence, consider the evidence and suggest an explanation.

2. Rocks under the Earth's surface can (at any point) be forced upwards to make mountains, a process known as uplift.
3. Erosion wears down rocks into sediment. The sediment is transported into a lake, river, or sea, where it is deposited at the bottom. Over a long period of time this will turn into sedimentary rock. Under the Earth's crust, the high temperatures and pressures may turn sedimentary rock (and igneous rock) into metamorphic rock. Some rocks sink lower and are hot enough to melt into magma. Some magma is forced out of volcanoes, solidifying and forming igneous rocks.

4.7 Using science to explain predictions: volcanoes

1. To ensure people can evacuate to safety in time.
2. To look for patterns to help make predictions about whether or not the volcano could erupt.
3. Gases such as sulfur dioxide escape from magma, the more gas there is suggests that the closer the magma is to the surface.

4.8 Soil

1. Rock fragments, air, water, humus.
2. Add water to the soil and shake. Allow the mixture to separate.
3. In clay soil, 40% of the rock fragments are clay, in sandy soil, most of the fragments are sand. Sandy soil feels gritty whilst clay soil feels sticky when wet and hard when dry. Sandy soil drains much faster than clay soil.
4. Sandy soil – the volume of water collected in 30 minutes was larger than the volume collected for the clay soil. Sandy soil drains quicker because the rock fragments are larger and there are more spaces for the water to drain through quickly.

4.9 More about soil

1. iron
2. Place 100 cm^3 of soil into a measuring cylinder, add water until it reaches 200 cm^3. Stir until there are no more bubbles. The difference between the volumes is the volume of air in the soil sample.
3. 200 cm^3 – 180 cm^3 = 20 cm^3

4.10 Fossils

1. Most dead animals and plants are eaten or rot. Fossils will only form if the animal is buried quickly.
2. An animal dies. It is buried in mud or sand. Bacteria slowly break down the soft parts of the body, leaving the skeleton. Mud or sand above the skeleton starts to become rock. Mineral-rich underground water seeps into tiny spaces in the skeleton, replacing the original minerals in the skeleton and creating a hard copy of the skeleton. When the soft rock is eroded, the fossil is exposed.
3. Students can choose any example on page 71 and do their own research on the find.

4.11 Estimating the age of the Earth

1 4 600 000 000 years old

2 Thomson assumed that the Earth formed as a liquid making his assumptions incorrect.

3 Index fossils are specific to the geological time period, so scientists can identify the age of the rock based on the fossils found within them.

4.12 Human fossils

1 Fossilised snails found nearby showed that the river Selam lived near flowed into a lake with sandy beaches.

2 The scientists used radiometric dating to date the surrounding rocks.

3 Toumaï's skull is not the same as modern gorillas, chimpanzees, or humans. Scientists cannot agree which species Toumaï is an ancestor of.

4.13 Review

1 Igneous, sedimentary, metamorphic.

2 Top to bottom: granite, sandstone, marble.

3a A, B

b A

c C, D

d A, B

e C, D

f A, B

4a V, W, X

b V

c X, there is marble (which is made from limestone) next to / below rock X.

d Under high temperatures and pressure.

e Y as it is the only igneous rock in the diagram.

5a 3

b Pumice has a low density (1), pumice contains bubbles (2).

c 3

d **i** I put it on water and it floated.

ii So it must have a low density.

6a hand lens

b B

c C

d Junaid, fossils are not very common, so it is very likely that a piece of sedimentary rock would not contain fossils.

7a M

b M

c L

d L

8a soil sample

b the water level

c the amount of soil used, the level to which water is added

9a Top to bottom: crust, mantle, outer core, inner core.

b Top to bottom: solid, solid, solid, liquid.

10 c, b, a, e, d

Stage 7 Review

1a solid

b melting

c The particles stop moving around from place to place. They arrange themselves in a regular pattern, and vibrate on the spot.

d **i** B

ii A

iii −7 °C

2a **i** temperature

ii

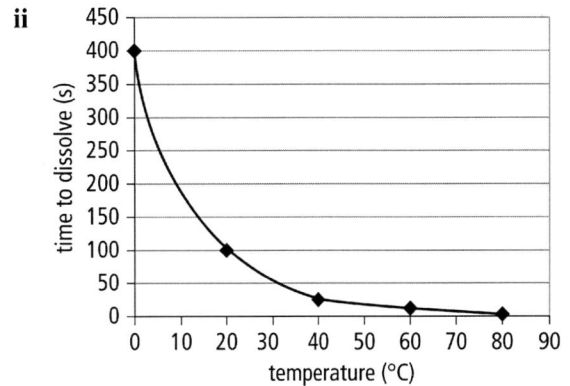

iii As the temperature of the water increases, the time taken for 20g of sugar to dissolve decreases.

b **i** Mass of sugar, temperature of water, volume of water.

ii The larger the size of the crystal, the longer it takes for the sugar to dissolve.

c big crystals

3 High melting point, good conductor of electricity, shiny, malleable, sonorous

4a Lake Victoria

b blue

c pH 7.8

d The pH would decrease.

e All three lakes are suitable.

5a Igneous rocks are formed from cooled magma.

b When rocks melt, forming magma, any fossils within the rocks are destroyed by the heat.

c Pumice, granite, basalt, gabbro, quartz.

6a All of the rocks contain fossils.

b A

c Mwamba quarry. Fossil F is the same as M. As G is below F, it must be older, therefore G is older than M.

d J

e The quarries are 1000 km apart and are on different continents, therefore it is possible that some rocks formed in one area and not the other.

f **i** Index fossils are fossils that are specific to a geological time frame and can therefore be used to date the age of the rock.

ii E, L

5 States of matter

5.1 The states of matter revisited

1 As in the liquid state diagram on page 80. Particles must be touching with very little space between them. Particles must not be arranged in a regular pattern e.g. lines.

2 Oxygen particles move randomly, without touching. The particles spread out to fill the whole container.

3 In the solid state the oxygen particles are touching without spaces between the particles. In the gas state, the particles do not touch and have spaces between them, allowing them to be compressed (pushed) together.

4 In a solid, the particles are arranged in a closely packed, regular pattern. Particles vibrate on the spot. In a liquid, the particles are touching with small amounts of empty spaces between them. The particles are not arranged in a regular pattern and they move around.

5 Liquid

5.2 Explaining diffusion

1 Diffusion is the random movement and mixing of particles.

2 Temperature, size and mass of the particles, the states of the substances that are diffusing.

3 Warmer particles have more energy so they move faster.

5.3 Explaining density

1 Density is how heavy something is for its size. (Density depends on the mass of the particles and how closely packed the particles are)

2 Density = $20 \div 2 = 10$ g/cm³

3 Tungsten. The table on page 85 shows that generally, as the relative mass of the metal increases, the density of the metal increases.

5.4 Explaining gas pressure

1 Particles colliding with the walls of a container.

2 As Shahid increases the amount of air particles (by pumping) the pressure inside the tyre increases.

3 As the air particles warm up in the pan, the particles move further apart and move faster, colliding with the walls of the bottle more often. This increase in pressure leads to the plastic bottle expanding/bulging/getting bigger.

4 82–84 Pa

5 For water to boil, the pressure of the water vapour must be equal to the air pressure. In Addis Ababa, as the air pressure is lower (due to the high altitude), the vapour pressure needed for the water to boil is lower than in Asmara where the air pressure is higher.

5.5 Ideas and evidence

1 An empirical question is a scientific question that requires an experiment or making observations to answer it.

2 Suggest explanations, test their explanations, check their evidence, think creatively about possible explanations.

3 Scientists collect evidence and make observations to test their explanations and help develop them.

4 Try to think of a different explanation, double check the evidence.

5.6 Doing an investigation

1 To keep the investigation fair and ensure that he is only measuring the effects of the variable he is changing (temperature).

2 As the volume of the gas increases, the pressure of the gas decreases at a decreasing rate.

3 Marcos's experiment collects data from a larger range than Azibo's.

5.7 Review

1

Property	Solid	Liquid	Gas
Volume	**fixed volume**	fixed volume	**same as container**
Shape	**fixed shape**	**same as container**	same as container
Can it flow?	**no**	yes	**yes**
Can it be compressed?	**no**	**slightly**	yes

2a boiling

b (1.5, 48)

c Incorrectly reading the thermometer, taking the thermometer out, incorrectly reading the time, not heating the liquid consistently.

3a Increase the temperature of the liquid.

b Students should draw a diagram similar to that of "particles of a substance in the gas state" on page 80.

c The particles would move around at a faster speed, not touching each other and moving apart to fill the container they were in.

4a the same as

b smaller than

c the same as

5

Property	Explanation
You cannot compress a solid.	The particles move around, in and out of each other.
If a gas is in a container with no lid, it escapes from the container.	There is no empty space between the particles.
A liquid takes the shape of the bottom of its container.	Its particles are in fixed positions.
A solid cannot be poured.	The particles move around in all directions.

6a The bromine vapour has diffused from one jar to the other.

b i At the lower temperature, the orange vapour would not have diffused as well between the two jars.

ii At a lower temperature, the gas particles have less energy and so move around less, slowing down the speed of diffusion.

7a 62 cm^3

b 69 − 62 = 7 cm^3

c 11.5 ÷ 7 = 1.64 g/cm^3

8a i substance that diffuses

ii distance from top of agar gel to bottom of colour

iii To ensure that none of the other variables affect the distance from top of agar to bottom of colour.

b Wear goggles, gloves, and ensure that she washes her hands after using potassium dichromate(VI).

c

Substance	Distance from top of agar to bottom of colour (cm)
Potassium manganate(VII)	
Copper sulfate	
Potassium dichromate(VI)	
Iodine	

d i To ensure that her results were reliable.

ii She may have left the experiment to run for different amounts of time.
She may have used different amounts of solid.

6 Material properties

6.1 Atoms

1 An atom is the smallest part of an element that can exist.

2 An element is a substance that cannot be split into anything simpler.

3 the same

4 different

6.2 Elements and their symbols

1 hydrogen: H, helium: He, lithium: Li, beryllium: Be, boron: B, carbon: C, nitrogen: N, oxygen: O, fluorine: F, neon: Ne.

2 Na: sodium, Mg: magnesium, Al: aluminium, Si: silicon, P: phosphorus, S: sulfur, Cl: chlorine, Ar: argon, K: potassium, Ca: calcium.

3 Platinum is silvery white, it conducts electricity, is shiny, and is not damaged by water or air. It is used for making jewellery, in hard drives, and in catalytic converters.

6.3 Discovering the elements

1 Sulfur, gold, and carbon exist naturally on their own, not joined to other elements

2 platinum (Pt), zinc (Zn), phosphorus (P), arsenic (As), bismuth (Bi)

3 rhenium and technetium

6.4 Organising the elements

1 Mendeleev used creative thinking to suggest an explanation.

2 Name of element, the properties, mass of one atom of the element.

3 Can scientists use patterns in properties to help find new elements?

4 Over time, Mendeleev's predictions were found to be correct.

6.5 Interpreting data from secondary sources

1 Oxygen, silicon, aluminium.

2 Haki is incorrect, the pie chart has "all other elements 1%", tin could be included in this amount.

3 As you go down the Group 1 elements, the melting points decrease. As you go down the Group 7 elements, the melting point increases.

6.6 Explaining differences between metals and non-metals

1 Melting point (high in metals, low in non-metals). Appearance (shiny in metals, dull in non-metals).

Ability to conduct electricity (metals are good conductors, non-metals are poor conductors except graphite).

Conductors of head (metals are good conductors, non-metals are poor conductors ex. diamond).

2 In a thin sheet of metal, the rows of atoms can slide over each other; whilst in non-metals, there are weak forces within the molecules that can be easily broken.

3 Chromium (a metal) has strong forces holding the atoms together which require lots of energy (a high temperature) to break, whilst argon (non-metal) has very weak forces existing between the atoms and requires relatively little energy (low temperature) to break.

6.7 What are compounds?

1 A compound is a substance that is made up of atoms of elements joined to atoms of other elements.

2 An element is made up of one type of atom, compounds are made up of at least two types of atoms (elements) joined together.

3a 1
 b 1
 c 2

4 At 20 °C carbon is a solid and oxygen is a colourless gas that you can't live without. At the same temperature, carbon monoxide is a toxic gas.

6.8 Making a compound

1 A hazard is a possible source of danger, a risk is the chance of damage or injury from a hazard.

2 Time, distance, shielding.

3 It is important to use scientific knowledge to explain and justify a conclusion to an investigation.

6.9 Naming compounds and writing formulae

1 copper sulfide: carbon and sulfur
silver bromide: silver and bromine
aluminium iodide: aluminium and iodine
iron sulfate: iron, sulfur, and oxygen
sodium carbonate: sodium, carbon, and oxygen
silicon dioxide: silicon and oxygen.

2 KCl: potassium chloride, ZnO: zinc oxide, SO_2: sulfur dioxide, SO_3: sulfur trioxide, $CuSO_4$: copper sulfate, $Pb(NO_3)_2$: lead nitrate

3 P_2O_5, $CaSO_4$

6.10 Oxides, hydroxides, sulfates, and carbonates

1 Calcium and oxygen, basic

2 Lithium, hydrogen, and oxygen.

3 Sodium, sulfur, and oxygen.

4 CaO: calcium oxide, SiO_2: silicon dioxide, KOH: potassium hydroxide, $Mg(OH)_2$: magnesium hydroxide, $CaCO_3$: calcium carbonate, Na_2SO_4: sodium sulfate

5 Magnesium oxide is used in furnaces as it has a very high melting point.

6.11 Chlorides

1 Potassium chloride

2 Using a table makes it easier to use the data in calculations, and keeps the data organised.

3 An average of the results is more accurate than just one result.

4 It is very difficult to evaporate all the water from the evaporating dish.

6.12 Mixtures

1 A mixture is a group of substances that are mixed up but not joined together.

2 Both compounds and mixtures have more than one type of atom, however, in a compound the atoms are joined together.

Mixtures can be separated into simpler substances easily, compounds cannot.

Compounds have different properties from the elements, whilst mixtures have the same properties as the substances that comprise it.

Amounts of the elements are always in the same ratio in compounds, whilst the amounts of substances can change in a mixture.

3 Mixtures: salt and water, stones and rice, sand and salad, iron nails and copper nails in a jar, air, iron and sulfur mix, orange juice.

Compounds: carbon dioxide, iron sulfide, any of the compounds on the previous pages or any reasonable compound.

4 A mixture of elements and compounds.

6.13 Separating mixtures – filtering and decanting

1 Students should draw something similar to the decanting and filtration diagrams on page 118.

2 Franco could decant the olive oil from the water.

3 Salty water contains salt dissolved in the water as a solution rather than a mixture. The salt particles are too small to be separated using the filter paper.

6.14 Separating mixtures – evaporation and distillation

1 Sodium chloride, lithium compounds

2 Evaporation removes the solvent from the solution (the water from the salt water) leaving the solute (salt) behind. Distillation would collect the water and leave the salt behind.

3 Place the ink solution into rounded-bottomed flask, heat the solution, cool the steam in the condenser, collect it in the beaker.

6.15 Separating mixtures – fractional distillation

1 Mixtures of liquids with different boiling points.

2 As the temperature of the fractioning column increases, the substance with the lower boiling point will evaporate first, leaving the fractioning column first and so condensing first.

3 Hexane

4 Russia, Saudi Arabia, USA

6.16 Separating mixtures – chromatography

1 Coloured compounds in leaves, dyes in ink. These are the only two options that are substances within a mixture of soluble substances.

2 The substance may dissolve better, one substance may stick to the chromatogram better. There are several possible answers.

3 Measure alcohol content in blood, look for explosives on body hair, identify nutrients in food.

6.17 Separating metals from their ores

1 During panning, the more dense substance falls to the bottom of the pan whilst the less dense substance can be mixed with water and removed.

2 Filtration and gravity.

3 It is heated with carbon and then melted.

4 1% of 100 kg = 1 kg of tin produced. 99 kg of waste would be produced.

5 China

6.18 What are you made of?

1 Hydrogen, oxygen, nitrogen, carbon.

2 Minerals are compounds that contain small amounts of other elements, such as iron and calcium.

3 You can suffer from tiredness, lack of energy, and shortness of breath.

4 Calcium deficiency: weak bones and frequent fractures.
Iodine deficiency: swelling of thyroid gland in neck, tiredness, brain damage.
Zinc deficiency: reduced growth in children, problems with senses and memory.

6.19 Review

1

Element	Chemical symbol
boron	B
beryllium	Be
silicon	**Si**
sodium	**Na**
sulfur	S
chlorine	**Cl**
fluorine	**F**
potassium	**K**

2 top to bottom: element, compound, element, element, compound, compound

3a 2, 4

 b 2, 4

 c 2, 4

4 When the metal is bent, the rows of atoms slide past each other, bending without breaking.

5a A, B, D

 b A, B, C, E

 c A

 d C

 e B

 f D

 g E

6 more than one, different from, are always the same, more than one, the same as, can vary.

7 Top to bottom:
calcium and oxygen
sodium and chlorine
potassium, hydrogen, and oxygen
iron, sulfur, and oxygen
magnesium, carbon, and oxygen

8a magnesium sulfate

 b sodium chloride

 c calcium carbonate

 d beryllium oxide

 e potassium hydroxide

9a Aluminium (Al), iron (Fe), calcium (Ca), sodium (Na), potassium (K), magnesium (Mg).

 b Aluminium

 c Oxygen and silicon

 d An element is only comprised of one type of element, a compound is comprised of different elements.

10a The second question is more specific and can be carried out in a school.

 b To let air (oxygen) into the crucible to allow the magnesium to continue reacting with the oxygen in the air.

 c Top to bottom:
–Wear appropriate clothing, stand back, do not lean over the crucible, have sand/fire extinguishers available.
–Do not look directly at the flame.

 d i 32.40 – 32.00 = 0.40 g of MgO
  ii 32.40 – 32.00 – 0.24 = 0.16 g of O_2

 e During the experiment, 0.16 g of oxygen reacted with 0.24 g of magnesium to form 0.40 g of magnesium oxide. The results show that as the magnesium burns, the mass increases.

7 Material changes

7.1 Chemical reactions

1 Chemical reactions create new substances, and are not reversible.

2 See flames, sparks, bubbles, notice a smell, feel the chemicals changing temperature, hear a noise.

3 Reactants: iron and oxygen.
Product is iron oxide.

4 The product (carbon dioxide) is a gas which escapes.

5 0.08 g of oxygen

7.2 Writing word equations
1 iron + sulfur → iron sulfide
2 calcium + oxygen → calcium oxide
3 reactants: copper oxide, hydrochloric acid
   products: copper chloride, water
4 magnesium + hydrochloric acid → magnesium chloride + hydrogen

7.3 Corrosion reactions
1 oxygen and water
2 iron + oxygen + water → hydrated iron oxide
3 Rust crumbles easily, leaving the underlying iron exposed to rust again. The cycle repeats, degrading the iron.
4 Coating iron in paint, another metal, or oil/grease prevents oxygen and water from reacting with the iron.

7.4 Doing an investigation
1 Seb: Variables to control: size and type of nail, volume of water used, temperature of the water.

   Variables to change: amount of salt added to the water

   Variable to observe: level of rust compared with the other nails.

   Seb could prepare 5 test tubes with 5 different solutions of salt water (1 g of salt per 10 ml, 2 g of salt per 10 ml etc). Once prepared, Seb could add a nail to each test tube. After 1 day, Seb could compare the levels of rust on the nails, concluding which solution of salt produced the rustiest nail.

   Students could draw something similar to the test tube diagram on page 138.

2 Tahlia: Apparatus list: 4 test tubes, 1 test tube rack, 4 iron nails (one painted, one greased, one coated with zinc, one left as a control), 4 bungs.

   Tahlia should place each nail in a test tube and cover with water before sealing with a bung. She should leave the nails for a day (or two) before comparing the amount of rust formed on each nail.

   Tahlia should ensure that all the variable should be kept the same (temperature, amount of water, type and size of nail etc).

7.5 Using reactions to identify chemicals
1 Dip the end of a clean nichrome wire into the compound that you are testing. Hold the end of the wire in a hot flame. Observe the flame colour.
2 sodium
3a green
 b aluminium hydroxide
4 iron(II) chloride + potassium hydroxide → iron(II) hydroxide + potassium chloride
   The iron(II) hydroxide forms a green precipitate.

7.6 Review
1a sodium + chlorine → **sodium chloride**
 b zinc + **oxygen** → zinc oxide
 c **iron** + sulfur → iron sulfide
 d iron + oxygen → **iron oxide**
 e carbon + **oxygen** → carbon dioxide
 f **sulfur** + oxygen → sulfur dioxide
2 react to make
3a Question ii is too broad as there are lots of possible factors that could speed up rusting. Question iii is more specific and would be easier to test.
 b i   amount of salt
   ii   how much of the nail has gone rusty
   iii size of salt crystals, volume of water
   iv To ensure that other factors do not interfere in the results of the experiment.
 c The nail is in contact with both air and water to be able to compare the amount of rust formed in the air and in the salty water and because both oxygen and water are needed to make rust.
 d Amount of salt added.
4a Reactants: sodium, iodine.
   Product: sodium iodide.
 b Reactants: carbon, oxygen.
   Product: carbon dioxide.
 c Reactants: sulfuric acid, copper oxide.
   Products: copper sulfate, water.
 d Reactants: magnesium, hydrochloric acid.
   Products: magnesium chloride, hydrogen.
 e Reactant: copper carbonate.
   Products: copper oxide, carbon dioxide.
5a sodium + bromine → sodium bromide
 b sulfur + oxygen → sulfur dioxide
 c calcium carbonate → calcium oxide + carbon dioxide
 d zinc + hydrochloric acid → zinc chloride + hydrogen
 e copper oxide + hydrochloric acid → copper chloride + water

6a-d

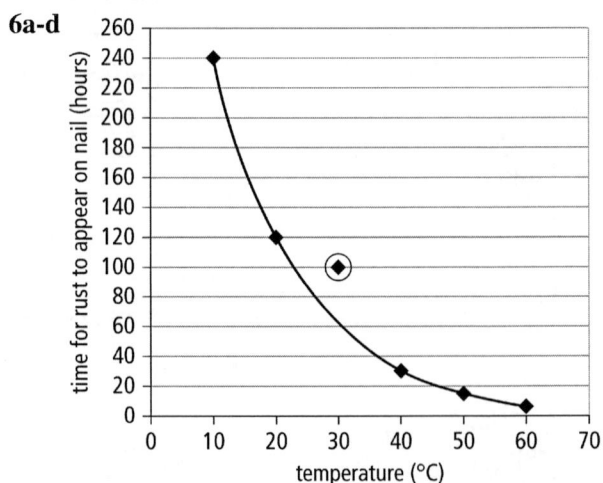

 e The measurements may not have been carried out correctly: the temperature could not have been measured correctly. Or the controlled variables may not have been kept the same.

7

Test tube number	Prediction	Reason for prediction
1	Nail will rust.	The nail is in contact with air and water.
2	Nail will not rust.	Paint prevents air and water being in contact with the nail.
3	Nail will not rust.	Grease prevents air and water being in contact with the nail.
4	Nail will not rust.	Magnesium is higher in the reactivity series than iron, so it reacts instead.
5	Nail will not rust.	The zinc coating prevent air and water being in contact with the iron.

Stage 8 review

1 gas
vibrate on the spot
close together
solid
liquid
move around, in and out of each other
a little
gas
much
move around from place to place

2

Name		Formula
carbon dioxide		He
copper sulfate		CO_2
carbon monoxide		N_2
nitrogen		$CuSO_4$
helium		CO

3a iron
b oxygen
c magnesium chloride
d oxygen
4a Diffusion is the random movement and mixing of particles.
b i lead and iodine
ii lead iodide
iii lead + iodine → lead iodide
c Reasons 1 and 4

d i temperature
ii time from adding crystals to formation of yellow solid
iii To ensure that none of the other variables influence the effects of the temperature (make the experiment fair).

e

Temperature (°C)	Time taken for precipitate to form (s)
20	60
30	30
40	15
50	14
60	3

f

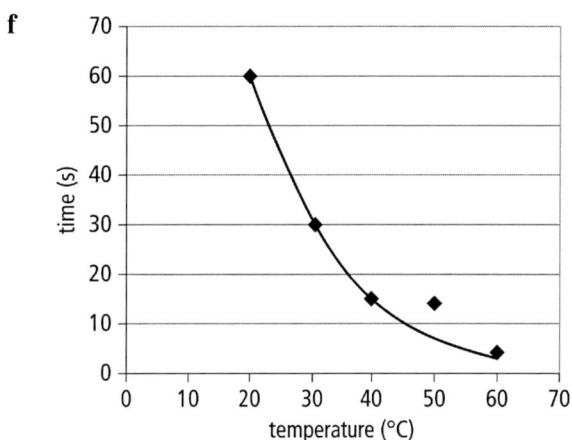

g As the temperature increases, the time taken for the precipitate to form decreases at a continually slowing rate.

h

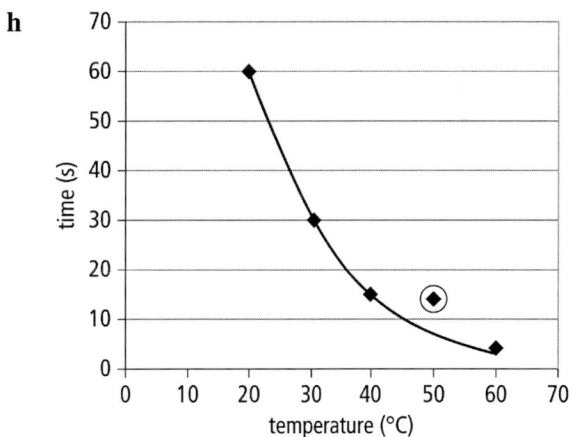

i Tamara should repeat the result to check if she made a mistake.
j As the temperature increases, the time taken for the precipitate to form decreases. At higher temperatures, particles have more energy and move around at a faster rate, decreasing the time it takes for a precipitate to form.

5a A, D, E
b B, C, F
c A, D, E
6 Density = 28/4 = 7 g/cm^3
7a calcium, gallium, zirconium, technetium
b bromine, gallium

8 Material properties

8.1 Atomic structure

1 Proton: charge +1, mass 1
Neutron: charge 0, mass 1
Electron: charge −1, mass 1/1840

2 Proton and neutron

3

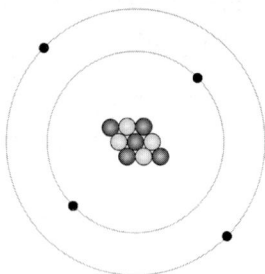

4 Beryllium has four protons with a total charge of +4 and four electrons with a total charge of −4. The net charge of the beryllium is 0 making it electrically neutral.

8.2 Finding electrons

1 When Thomson passed cathode rays between electrically charged pieces of metal, the rays bent towards the positively charged metal, suggesting that they are negatively charged.

2 Thomson's plum pudding model suggests that electrons are placed within a positively charged sphere (like plums dotted throughout a plum pudding). Nagaoka's Saturn model suggests that the atom has a large positive mass at the centre with negative charges surrounding the positive mass in rings.

3 Nagaoka said that it is not possible for negative charges to be spread through a positively charged sphere.

8.3 Discovering the nucleus

1 Rutherford's model of the atom suggests that most of the mass of an atom is in a nucleus in the centre of the atom. The nucleus is positively charged. Surrounding the nucleus is a big, empty space in which electrons move.

2 Rutherford, Geiger, and Marsden fired positive alpha particles at a thin piece of gold foil. A fluorescent screen surrounded the foil to record where the alpha particles collided with the screen, allowing Rutherford to determine whether or not the particles had changed direction.

3 By firing positive particles into the air, Rutherford found that tiny positive particles were formed from the nuclei of nitrogen atoms. These tiny positive particles were protons.

8.4 Protons, electrons, and the periodic table

1 Students should copy the lithium, sodium, and potassium diagrams on page 153. All three atoms have 2 electrons in the first shell and 1 electron in the outer shell.

2 Helium: 2, neon: 2,8, argon: 2,8,8. Helium, neon, and argon have 2 electrons in the inner shells. Both neon and argon have 8 electrons in the outer shells.

3 Lithium: 2,1, beryllium: 2,2, boron: 2,3, carbon: 2,4, nitrogen: 2,5, oxygen: 2,6, fluorine: 2,7, neon: 2,8. The number of electrons in the outer shell of the elements increase (by one) as you move across the periodic table.

8.5 Proton number, nucleon number, and isotopes

1 Isotopes are atoms of the same element with different number of neutrons.

2 proton number: 15, nucleon number: 31

3 19 protons, 20 neutrons

8.6 The Group 1 elements

1 As you move down Group 1, the melting point of the metals decreases.

2 Generally, as you move down Group 1, the density of the metals increases. Potassium does not fit the pattern.

3 Group 1 element + water → Group 1 hydroxide + hydrogen. e.g sodium + water → sodium hydroxide + hydrogen. As you move down the group, the reactions become more vigorous.

8.7 The Group 2 elements

1 calcium + water → calcium hydroxide + hydrogen
strontium + water → strontium hydroxide + hydrogen
barium + water → barium hydroxide + hydrogen

2 Beryllium is at the top of group 2. The reactions get more vigorous as you move down the group. As beryllium is at the top of the group, it would be the least reactive (far less reactive than calcium).

3 Set up the apparatus as shown on page 159. Place a piece of magnesium in the bottom of a test tube. Repeat with a piece of beryllium of the same size. Put some dilute hydrochloric acid into the test tube and observe the reaction. Whichever metal produces more hydrogen bubbles is more vigorous.

8.8 The Group 7 elements

1 Group 7 elements have low melting and boiling points compared to most metals. As you move down the group, the melting and boiling points increase. This is because the atoms (and molecules) of the elements get bigger as you move down the group.

2 iron + chlorine → iron chloride
iron + bromine → iron bromide
iron + iodine → iron iodide
Moving down the group the reactions get less vigorous.

8.9 Looking at secondary data – chlorinating water

1 By asking many people, the data is more reliable and other scientists would be more likely to trust the scientist's results.

2 The scientists may not have been able to find any more people.

It would have been more expensive to question more people.

There may have been time limits on the study.

Any reasonable answer is acceptable.

3 The benefits of adding chlorine (reducing deaths from waterborne diseases) outweigh the possible risk of cancers.

8.10 Periodic trends

1 lithium, beryllium, boron, carbon, nitrogen, oxygen, fluorine, neon

2 Vipasa does not have the equipment or the metals available.

3 Generally, as you move across period 3 (left to right), the melting points increase, peaking at silicon and then decreases very quickly.

8.11 How scientists work: inside sub-atomic particles

1 Scientists can divide up the tasks and work separately to solve problems faster.

The best scientists available from each country can work together.

2 Time differences, language barriers.

3 Modern technology such as telephones, Internet, and readily available international transport.

8.12 Review

1 Clockwise from top: electron, neutron, nucleus.

2

Sub-atomic particle	Charge	Relative mass
proton	+1	1
neutron	0	1
electron	−1	1/1840

3 There are the same number of protons (15) and electrons (15). The positive charge of the protons (+15) neutralises the negative charge of the electrons (−15).

4a Most of an atom is empty space (between the electrons and the nucleus), so the positive alpha particles travelled straight through.

b Some of the positive alpha particles hit the positive nucleus and bounced (were repelled) backwards.

5a See diagram on page 153.

b See diagram on page 153.

c See diagram on page 153.

6a sodium: 2,8,1
potassium: 2,8,8,1

b Both sodium and potassium have 2 electrons in the inner shell and 8 electrons in the middle shells.

c Sodium and potassium are in Group 1 and both have 1 electron in the outer shell.

7a

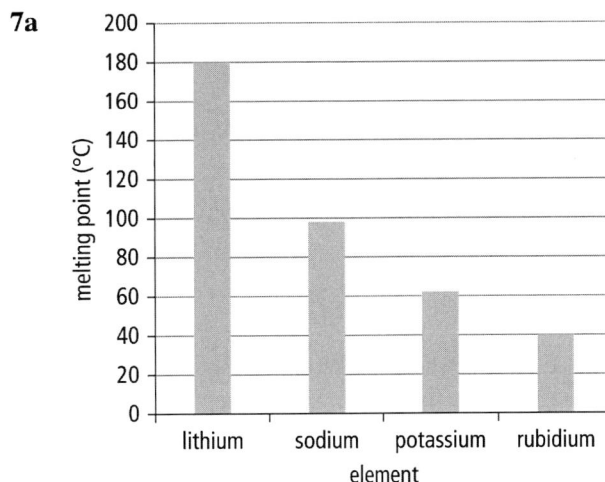

b As you move down the group, the melting point decreases.

8a The bubbles show that hydrogen is being produced.

b The sodium hydroxide that is formed is alkaline.

c sodium + water → sodium hydroxide + hydrogen

d **i** Hydrogen is produced. An alkaline solution is produced.

ii The reaction of potassium is more vigorous.

e As you move down Group 1, the reactions become more vigorous.

9a The relative size of the atom increases down the group.

b The number of electron shells increases (as you move down the group), increasing the relative size of the atom.

10a As you move down Group 2 (beryllium to strontium), the boiling point decreases.

b Barium would have a lower boiling point.

c Prediction: the melting point would decrease as you move down the group. Reason: the boiling point decreases, suggesting that the melting point would too.

11a variable to change: element
variable to observe: how vigorous the reaction is

b the amount of element used, the temperature of the water

c Collect data about the reactions and the amount of chemicals to use. Carry out a risk assessment.

d The reaction of strontium with water is very vigorous and can be dangerous.

12a Two of: fluorine, chlorine, bromine, iodine, astatine.

b do not conduct electricity, poor conductors of heat

c **i** bromine

ii As you move down the group the boiling point increases.

iii Approximately −101 °C

d See images on page 161.

13a magnesium: 2,8,2
aluminium: 2,8,3
silicon: 2,8,4
phosphorus: 2,8,5
sulfur: 2,8,6

chlorine: 2,8,7

argon: 2,8,8

  b sodium, magnesium, aluminium

  c phosphorus, sulfur, chlorine, argon, (silicon is a semiconductor)

  d As you move across the period (left to right) the relative size of the atoms decreases.

9   Energy changes

9.1   Energy changes in chemical reactions

1   Burning a fuel, neutralisation reactions

2   Melting and evaporating

3   Dissolving

4   When a reaction releases energy, the energy heats up the mixture before being transferred to the surroundings, increasing the temperature.

9.2   Investigating fuels

1   Fatima repeats her investigation to make sure her results are reliable and reduce errors.

2   The average temperature change for ethanol was the lowest value.

3   The question is not specific enough/too open ended.

9.3   Choosing fuels

1   A fuel is a substance that releases useful heat when it burns.

2   hydrogen: water

ethanol: carbon dioxide and water

3

Fuel	Advantage	Disadvantage
Ethanol	Made from a renewable source (sugar cane). Liquid at room temperature. Convenient to transport and store.	Produces carbon dioxide (a greenhouse gas). Sugar cane is grown instead of food reducing food production.
Hydrogen	Only product is water. Made from a renewable source (methane). Releases 3 times more energy per gram than diesel and almost 5 times more than ethanol.	Hydrogen is difficult to store and transport. Hydrogen is highly explosive.
Diesel	From a non-renewable source. Liquid at room temperature. Convenient to transport and store.	Produces carbon dioxide (a greenhouse gas) and small products that can increase the risk of cancer or heart disease.

9.4   Calculating food energy

1 $H = m \times c \times \Delta T$

$H = 1 \times 4.2 \times (80-20)$

$H = 252$ J

2   Some of the heat released from the food would have been transferred to the surroundings rather than the water

3   Temperature is a measure of how hot or cold something is. Heat is a type of energy that can be transferred from one thing to another.

9.5   Investigating endothermic changes

1   Variable to change: volume of solvent

Variable to observe: temperature change (the greater the temperature change, the greater the amount of heat taken in)

Variable to control: substance used, mass of solute

2a   Decide on which substances to use, decide on the volume of water to use, choose the equipment they need to use.

  b

Substance	Temperature change (°C)

9.6   Review

1   given out, increases, taken in, decreases

2

Type of change	Is the change exothermic?	Is the change endothermic?
combustion (burning)	✓	
neutralisation	✓	
evaporation		✓
melting		✓
freezing	✓	

3a   copper sulfate

  b   potassium nitrate

4a   The reaction is endothermic, taking in energy (heat) from the surrounding area, reducing the temperature of the water, causing it to freeze.

  b   Endothermically, the surrounding area gets cooler (the water freezes) demonstrating that heat has been taken in (an endothermic reaction).

5a   56 − 23 = 33 °C

  b   An increase in temperature shows that heat has been given out. Exothermic reactions give out heat.

6a   fuel

  b   temperature change

  c   the amount of fuel, the temperature of the water at the start, the distance between the spirit burner and the calorimeter

  d   The temperature change in large/small volumes would be harder to measure and less accurate.

  e   **i**   propanol/temperature at start: 20 °C

        butanol/temperature change: 45 °C

    ii   ethanol

f To improve the reliability of her results.

g the surroundings

7a To reduce the chance of error and to improve reliability.

b The result is not consistent with the other results.

c The neutralisation reactions are all exothermic. The hydrochloric acid and potassium hydroxide reaction is the most exothermic.

10 The reactivity series

10.1 The reactions of metals with oxygen

1 Bright white flame and crackling sounds.

2 iron oxide

3 zinc + oxygen → zinc oxide

4 magnesium, iron, copper

10.2 The reactions of metals with water

1 potassium, sodium, lithium, calcium

2 Products: potassium hydroxide and hydrogen
Potassium + water → potassium hydroxide + hydrogen

3 Gold does not react with cold water.

10.3 The reactions of metals with acids

1 potassium, sodium, lithium, calcium.

2 Products: magnesium chloride and water
magnesium + hydrochloric acid → magnesium chloride + water

3 Collect the hydrogen in a test tube. Put a lit splint into the test tube. The splint makes a squeaky pop and goes out.

4 To ensure that there is the same amount of metal free to react, allowing him to compare the results.

10.4 The reactivity series

1 More reactive: potassium, sodium, lithium, calcium. Less reactive: aluminium, zinc, iron, lead, copper, silver, gold.

2 The potassium would react violently with dilute acid.

3 Magnesium, like zinc, is more reactive than steel. The magnesium reacts with the water instead of the iron in the steel, thus protecting the boat's steel hull.

10.5 Nickel in the reactivity series

1 Priti used secondary sources because the tests were too hazardous for her to carry out herself.

2 When reacting with oxygen, all of the metals formed oxides quickly. There was no clear difference in the speeds of the reactions.

3 Priti has one piece of evidence to suggest that nickel is higher in the reactivity series than lead. To be confident, Priti needs to collect more evidence supporting this conclusion.

10.6 Metal displacement reactions

1 A displacement reaction is a reaction in which one element displaces (pushes out) another element from its compound.

2 magnesium + copper oxide → magnesium oxide + copper
zinc + magnesium oxide → No reaction
zinc + copper sulfate solution → zinc sulfate + copper

3 aluminium + iron oxide → aluminium oxide + iron. This reaction is known as the thermite reaction. The thermite reaction is used to produce liquid iron to join railway tracks together.

10.7 Using the reactivity series: extracting metals from their ores

1 potassium, sodium, calcium, magnesium, aluminium

2 Most iron exists in the Earth's crust as iron oxide. Carbon is more reactive than iron, so can displace the iron from the iron oxide to produce iron.

3 Metals near the top of the reactivity series are extracted using electrolysis, whilst metals below aluminium are extracted from their oxides by heating with carbon.

10.8 Writing symbol equations

1 $4Na + O_2 → 2Na_2O$

2 $Zn(s) + CuSO_4(aq) → ZnSO_4(aq) + Cu(s)$

3 $K(s) + H_2O(l) → KOH(aq) + H_2(g)$

10.9 Review

1a magnesium + oxygen → magnesium oxide

b zinc + oxygen → zinc oxide

c potassium + oxygen → potassium oxide

2a sodium

b iron, zinc, magnesium, sodium

c no reaction

d No reaction, platinum is unreactive in water, dilute acids, or oxygen.

e magnesium, zinc (sodium is incorrect as it reacts vigorously with water)

3a hydrogen

b Add Universal Indicator, the solution would turn blue/purple.

c lithium hydroxide

d potassium + water → potassium hydroxide

e potassium, lithium, magnesium

f sodium

g Potassium and lithium react violently with dilute acids.

4a **i** the metal

ii Amount of dilute hydrochloric acid and the amount of metal added.

iii To ensure that they are the only variables influencing the results (to make it a fair test).

b Half fill the test tubes with dilute hydrochloric acid. To each test tube, add either a spatula of iron, zinc, or 1 cm of magnesium ribbon. Observe the reactions.

c

Metal	Reaction
iron	
zinc	
magnesium	

d To determine whether the type of acid affects the reaction.

e Collect the gas produced in a test tube. Place a lit splint inside. If the splint makes a squeaky pop and goes out, there is hydrogen present.

5a ii and iii will react

b lead + copper oxide → lead oxide + copper
zinc + lead oxide → zinc oxide + lead

6a copper, zinc sulfate

b The zinc has displaced the copper.

c i Zinc is more reactive as it displaces the nickel.
ii zinc + nickel nitrate → zinc nitrate + nickel
iii There would be no reaction as nickel is less reactive than zinc.

7a i Zinc is more reactive than iron, lead, and tin.
ii A metal cannot displace itself, so it would be a waste of resources.

b Tin is less reactive than iron and zinc, but more reactive than lead.

c Mary could add lead to tin chloride to see if there is a reaction.

11 Making salts – acids and metals

11.1 Making salts – acids and metals
1 Filtration removes the metal from the solution.
2 zinc + hydrochloric acid → zinc chloride + hydrogen
3 magnesium metal + nitric acid

11.2 Making salts – acids and carbonates
1 evaporation
2 zinc carbonate + hydrochloric acid → zinc chloride + carbon dioxide + water
3 zinc carbonate + nitric acid

11.3 Making salts – acids and alkalis
1 Add charcoal to the solution, then filter the solution.
2 potassium hydroxide + nitric acid → potassium nitrate + water
The salt made is potassium nitrate.
3 potassium hydroxide + hydrochloric acid

11.4 Making salts – fertilisers
1 ammonium nitrate
2 evaporation

11.5 Review
1 A compound made when a metal replaces the hydrogen in an acid.
2a magnesium sulfate
b zinc chloride
c magnesium nitrate
d copper chloride
e zinc sulfate
f copper nitrate
3a Collect the hydrogen gas, place a lit splint inside. If the splint makes a squeaky 'pop' and goes out, the gas is hydrogen.
b bubbles forming
4a magnesium nitrate + hydrogen
b zinc sulfate + hydrogen
c magnesium chloride + hydrogen
d copper chloride + carbon dioxide + water
e zinc nitrate + water
5a sulfuric acid
b i copper sulfate + carbon dioxide + water
ii copper carbonate + sulfuric acid → copper sulfate + carbon dioxide + water
iii copper sulfate + water
iv copper oxide + sulfuric acid → copper sulfate + water
c i copper sulfate, water, copper oxide
ii filtration
d Transfer the solution into the evaporating dish. Using the beaker set up a water bath with the evaporating dish on top. Gently heat the beaker, evaporating the water in the evaporating dish, leaving copper sulfate crystals behind.
6a i carbon dioxide
ii copper carbonate + hydrochloric acid → copper chloride + carbon dioxide + water
b A, D, F, B, E, C, G, H
7a zinc + hydrochloric acid → zinc chloride + hydrogen
b i Dilute hydrochloric acid can cause harm in cuts.
ii The reaction releases hydrogen which is extremely flammable.
iii Dilute hydrochloric acid and zinc chloride crystals/concentrated solution can damage the eye.
iv Zinc chloride crystals and concentrated solutions of zinc chloride are corrosive and will burn the skin.
c Heating the evaporating dish over a water bath heats the zinc chloride more evenly and gently, reducing spitting and reducing the loss of zinc chloride.

12 Rates of reaction

12.1 Rates of reaction
1 Very fast reaction: the chemical reaction in fireworks. Very slow reaction: rust forming on a car.
2 55 cm^3
3 The graph evens out and continues horizontally.

12.2 Concentration and reaction rates
1 It is easier to compare or see a trend or pattern in continuous data by using a line graph.
2 As the concentration of the acid increases, the reaction rate increased.
3 In a more concentrated solution, there is a greater number of acid particles that can react with the magnesium particles, increasing the rate of the reaction.
4 The student could use the same method to test equivalent concentrations of different acids.

12.3 Temperature and reaction rates
1 The higher the temperature, the faster the rate of reaction.
2 At higher temperatures, particles have more energy so move around faster. This increase in movement leads to an increase in collisions between reacting particles, leading to an increase in rate of reaction.
3 Farai could time how long it takes for a 5 cm piece of magnesium to stop reacting in hydrochloric acid at different temperatures.

12.4 Surface area and reaction rates
1 Temperature, amount of dilute hydrochloric acid, total amount of calcium carbonate used.
2 The greater the surface area, the faster the rate of reaction.
3 One gram of solid has a much smaller surface area than one gram of powdered solid. During a reaction, the reactants can only act with the surface of the solid. As the powder has a greater surface area, more reactions are able to take place, speeding up the rate of reaction.

12.5 Catalysts and reaction rates
1 Catalysts speed up reactions without being used up in the reaction.
2 Salivary amylase, catalase (from liver), manganese(IV) oxide, lead(IV) oxide, iron, catalytic converters (platinum, rhodium, palladium).
3 Catalysts make it easier for the reaction to start.

12.6 Review
1a zinc + hydrochloric acid → zinc chloride + hydrogen
 b i Between 0 and 1 minute.
  ii 3 minutes
  iii 80 cm^3

c i amount of zinc used, temperature, amount of acid used
 ii To ensure that any results are caused by the change of concentration of acid (make it a fair test).
 iii

Concentration of acid	Amount of gas produced (cm³)

2a i temperature
 ii time taken for the cross to disappear
 iii amount of sodium thiosulfate, amount of hydrochloric acid, concentration of sodium thiosulfate, concentration of hydrochloric acid, temperature
 b i To reduce error and increase the reliability of his results.
  ii 200
  iii

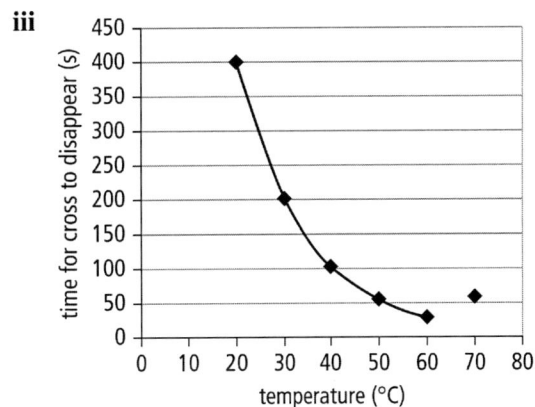

 iv

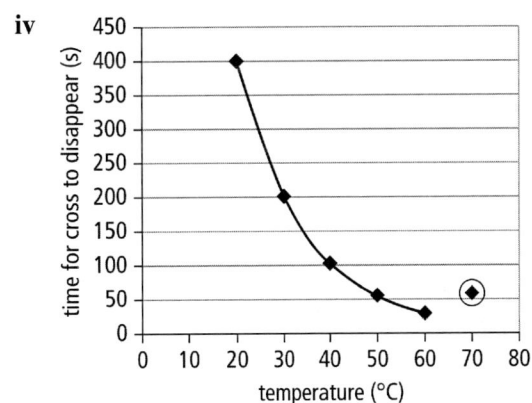

 v As temperature increases, the time taken for the cross to disappear decreases.
 c At higher temperatures, particles have more energy so move around faster. This increase in movement leads to an increase in collisions between reacting particles, leading to and increase in rate of reaction.

3a carbon dioxide

b **i** The product that is formed as gas escapes into the air.

ii B

c **i** size of calcium carbonate – surface area

ii time taken for 1.0 g of gas to be made

iii the amount of calcium carbonate, temperature, amount of hydrochloric acid

iv

Size of calcium carbonate	Time taken for 1.0 g of gas to be produced
big lumps	
small lumps	
powder	

v For a certain mass of calcium carbonate, the powder has the biggest surface area.

4a A catalyst is a chemical that helps to speed up a reaction without being used up.

b

Catalyst	Volume of gas produced (cm³)

Stage 9 review

1a 7

b protons and neutrons

c Group 1

2a There is a large amount of space between the nucleus and the electrons, the positively charged particles could pass through here.

b nucleus

c Most of an atom is empty space through which the positive particles can travel. Only a small number change direction.

3a C

b A and D

c D

4a

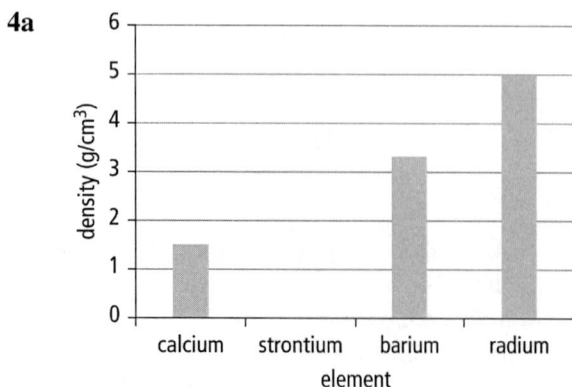

b Approximately 2.5 g/cm³

5a Table A: Group 1

Table B: Group 7

b As you move down the group, the boiling points decrease.

c As you move down the group, the boiling points increase (opposite to the elements in table A).

6a There is an increase in temperature.

b combustion, freezing

7a variable he changes: fuel

variable he measures: temperature change

b the amount of water, the amount of fuel used, the distance between the burner and the calorimeter

c **i** Missing value for pentanol is 12. Missing value for heptanol is 42.

ii hexanol

d No, Artem's conclusion is not correct. The fuels released different amounts of heat when they burned.

8a calcium and zinc oxide

lead and copper sulfate solution

b calcium + zinc oxide → calcium oxide + zinc

lead + copper sulfate → lead sulfate + copper

c **i** Gold is very unreactive and will stay shiny.

ii Calcium reacts quickly with water.

iii Sodium is very reactive.

9a copper chloride

b magnesium sulfate

c zinc nitrate

10a calcium + water → calcium hydroxide + hydrogen

b magnesium + oxygen → magnesium oxide

c zinc + hydrochloric acid → zinc chloride + water

11a To remove the remaining zinc from the solution.

b Zara can transfer the zinc chloride into an evaporating dish and heat over a water bath to make zinc chloride crystals.

1 States of matter

1.1 The Particle theory of matter

1 particles, identical, liquid, states, move around from place to place, weak

2a See the diagram of a solid on p14 of the Student book. All of the particles should be touching each other in a regular arrangement.

b Particles in a solid don't move around and vibrate on the spot.

3 More of the particles should be touching each other. Improved diagram should show the particles randomly arranged, as here, but with more of them touching each other.

4 Solids only – statements C, E, G
Gases only – statement H
Solids and liquids – statements F, I
Liquids and gases – statement B
Solids, liquids, and gases – statements A, D, J

Extension
A piece of cake contains particles in both the solid state and the gas state. Most of the cake is in a solid state, but there are bubbles of air throughout the cake, which are in the gas state.

1.2 Boiling, evaporating, and condensing

1a F – Condensation is the change of state from gas to liquid.

b T

c F – When a substance changes state from liquid to gas, the forces of attraction between its particles get weaker.

d T

e F – When a substance condenses, the forces of attraction between its particles get stronger.

2a D

b B

c D and C

3

	True of evaporation only	True of boiling only	True of both evaporation and boiling
This involves a change of state from a substance in its liquid state.			✔
Particles leave the surface of the liquid only.	✔		
Bubbles of the substance in its gas state form throughout the liquid.		✔	
This can happen at any temperature.	✔		
During this change of state, the particles get further apart.			✔

1.3 Questions, evidence, and explanations

1 Top to bottom:
ask a question, suggest an explanation, test the explanation, check the evidence

2 Top to bottom:
Evidence, evidence, explanation, evidence, evidence, evidence, explanation

3a How does the amount of salt added to water affect the boiling temperature?

b The saltier the water, the higher the boiling temperature.

c Laura could add different amounts (1 g, 2 g etc.) of salt to a fixed volume of water (e.g. 100 cm³) and measure the boiling temperature.

1.4 Melting, freezing, and subliming

1 solid, liquid, move out of, move around, are touching their neighbours.

2 From left to right:
Sloping part of graph on left – C; horizontal part of graph – A; sloping part of graph on right – B

3a sodium

b Sodium, lead, copper, manganese, iron, chromium.

c copper

4a i water
ii mercury

b Scale drawn with equal divisions from approximately −120 °C up to −360 °C.

c Melting and boiling points correctly marked on scale.

d i Chlorine is in the gas state, ethanol is in the liquid state.
ii mercury

1.5 Energy and changes of state

1 A, F, B, D, C, E

2a

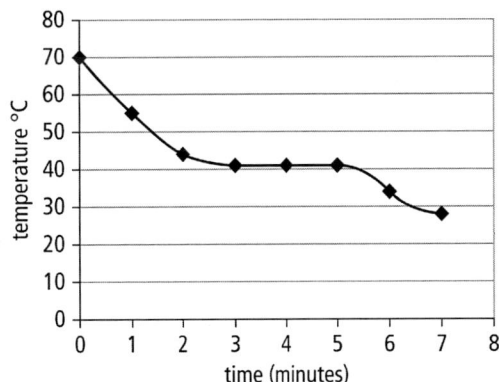

b 41 °C

c i Label at the plateau (41 °C).
ii Label at the first part of the curve (0,70) to (2,44).
iii Label at the last part of the curve (6,34) to (7,28).

Extension:

a It takes time for energy to leave the water, and go the water particles to arrange themselves into a pattern.

b Water particles in sweat take heat energy away from the body when they evaporate, cooling it down.

c The particles in water need energy (from heating) to overcome the forces holding them together.

1.6 Using particle theory to explain dissolving

1

Word	Meaning
solute	The process of adding a solid to a liquid so that you can no longer see separate pieces of solid.
solvent	A substance that is dissolved in a liquid.
solution	A substance is _____ in a liquid if it dissolves in the liquid.
dissolving	The mass of a substance that dissolves in 100 g of water.
soluble	A liquid in which another substance dissolves.
insoluble	A substance is _____ in a liquid if it does not dissolve in the liquid.
solubility	A mixture of a liquid and dissolved substance.

2 A

3 250 + 10 = 260 g

Extension:

Student	Correct, incorrect, or partly correct
Kamol	Partly correct: stirring makes the particles move faster, however if the solution is saturated, no more copper sulfate will dissolve.
Lawan	Correct: if no more copper sulfate will dissolve, they have made a saturated solution.
Mongkut	Correct: increasing the energy of the water would allow more copper sulfate to dissolve.
Niran	Correct: you can use filter paper and a filter to remove any undissolved solids.
Pakpao	Incorrect: if the copper sulfate has dissolved, it cannot be removed by filtration.
Ratana	Correct: increasing the energy of the water would allow more copper sulfate to dissolve.
Sunan	Correct: using evaporation would cause copper sulfate crystals to grow if left long enough.

1.7 Planning an investigation

1a top to bottom: change, control, measure

b **i** measuring cylinder

   ii laboratory thermometer (not clinical)

c 58 cm^3

Extension:

Measure out 100 cm^3 of water and pour it into a beaker.

Measure the temperature of the water.

Add salt, 1g at a time, with stirring.

When no more will dissolve, write down the mass of the salt added.

Measure out a fresh sample of 100 cm^3 of water and pour it into a beaker.

Heat the water to 40 °C.

Add salt, 1 g at a time, with stirring

When no more will dissolve, write down the mass of the salt added.

1.8 Presenting evidence

1

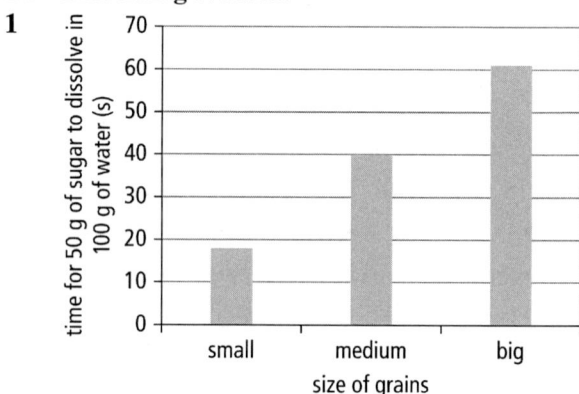

2a

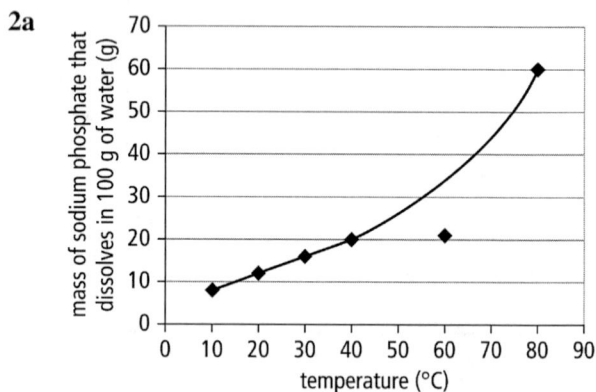

b iv

Extension:

Temperature (°C)	Copper sulfate	Sodium carbonate	Potassium chloride

2 Material properties

2.1 Introducing elements

1a T

b F – An element is a substance that cannot be split up to make other substances.

c F – There are 92 elements that are found naturally on Earth.

d T

e T

2 gold, copper, iodine, oxygen, chlorine

3 metals: lithium, manganese, nickel, rhodium, tungsten, vanadium, yttrium

non-metals: oxygen, phosphorus, sulfur, xenon, zirconium

4a hydrogen and helium

b oxygen and silicon

c nitrogen

Extension:

Anything appropriates

2.2 Metal elements

1 Metal properties – sonorous, shiny, hard, high melting point, good conductor of heat, strong, good conductor of electricity, ductile, high density, malleable.

2 Water pipes – waterproof, high melting point, malleable

Bells – sonorous

Bicycle frames – shiny, hard, high melting point, strong, malleable

Electric cables – ductile, high melting point, good conductor of electricity, strong

Cooking pans – shiny, high melting point, good conductor of heat, strong

Coins – shiny, hard, high melting point, strong

3 A, C, and E are likely to be metals because they have high melting and boiling points, and high density values.

4 Ways in which lithium, sodium, and potassium are like other metals – they are shiny, and good conductors of electricity.

Way in which lithium, sodium, and potassium are not like other metals – they are soft.

2.3 Non-metal elements

1 Typical metals tend to have high melting and boiling points, whilst typical non-metals have low melting and boiling points. Typical metals are good conductors of both electricity and heat and are shiny. Typical non-metals are poor conductors of electricity and heat and are usually dull looking.

2 C and E are non-metals.

3a Carbon (as diamond) does not conduct electricity.

b Its melting point is higher than 3500 °C and its boiling point is 4827 °C.

Extension:

a Germanium is shiny.

b Germanium is brittle and has poor electrical conductivity.

c Yes, it has both metal and non-metal characteristics. If no, ensure the student has a valid point.

2.4 Making conclusions from data

1a D, F, C, A, E, B

b A, B, E

2a I, L, K, J, G, H

b G, H, J. All three have a high melting point, conduct electricity, and are shiny.

c K, this element cannot conduct electricity but is shiny and silver coloured.

Extension:

a Metals conduct heat much better than non-metals

b The conclusions should say that elements with high thermal conductivity are often metals.

2.5 Metal alloys

1 Low density, stiff, hard, shiny, strong, is not damaged by air and water.

2 The best material for the job is the alloy in column C.

3 Benefits – better than aluminium alloy because it is harder, stronger when pulled, stiffer and has a greater fatigue strength.

Bar chart – name of material on X-axis; property name and units on Y-axis; Y-axis scale drawn with equal divisions.

Disadvantage compared with old aluminium alloy – the new alloy has a greater density. But the added strength of a bicycle made from the new alloy outweighs its extra mass.

2.6 Material properties

1 stiff, strong

2a good conductor of heat, rigid, waterproof

b poor conductor of heat, rigid

c good conductor of electricity, flexible

d poor conductor of heat, flexible

Extension:

a To ensure that the material does not melt when the processors get hot.

b Copper has the highest thermal conductivity and has a high melting point.

c Copper is the most dense and would add weight to the computer.

d Aluminium alloy 6063 is the hardest material and isn't very dense.

2.7 Polymers

1 Buckets, bottles, plates, bags etc (anything reasonable).

2 long, difficult, flexible

3 Pipes: waterproof – prevents water from leaking out of the pipe.

Insulation: does not conduct electricity – protects the surrounding areas from electricity.

Waterproof clothes: waterproof, flexible – keeps the wearer dry and comfortable.

Roofing for houses: flexible, waterproof, does not catch fire easily – roofing needs to be protective, keeping the inhabitants dry and safe from fire.

4a Poly(butene) is suitable for making water pipes because it is not damaged by hot water.

b Poly(butene) is not used to transport water that has had chlorine added to it because it is damaged by chlorine and substances that contain chlorine.

3 Material changes

3.1 Acids and alkalis

1 Acidic substances: limes, lemons, vinegar, vitamin C, fish oils,

Alkaline substances: toothpaste, washing powder.

2 hydrochloric

sulfuric

nitric

sodium hydroxide

3a The last symbol.

b wear gloves and goggles

4a making other chemicals

b 14% is used for soap, detergents, and textiles.

c 7.14 million tonnes

3.2 The pH scale and indicators

1a T

b F – The pH of an alkaline solution is more than 7

c F – The more acidic a solution, the lower its pH.

d T

e T

f T

2 The unknown solution is alkaline. When indicator is added the colour is the same as for sodium hydroxide, which is known to be alkaline.

3 Make indicators from each of the species' petals in turn: add petals to water, heat the mixture, filter, and collect the filtrate.

Test each indicator in turn by adding a few drops to acidic, alkaline, and neutral solutions. If the colour of an indicator is different in two or more of the three solutions, then the species' petals make a suitable indicator.

Extension:

a Solution A is more concentrated since a greater mass of sodium hydroxide is dissolved in the same volume of solution.

b She could dissolve any mass greater than 40 g.

3.3 Neutralisation

1 purple, alkaline, decreases, 7, neutralised, decreases, red

2a F – The lakes are neutralised by adding alkali.

b T

c F – The pH increases.

d T

e F – The pH stays the same, the concentration changes.

3 The last table. Students should plot a graph with points at (0, 1) and (20, 7).

3.4 Planning investigations and collecting evidence

1a By answering the question, the students will know the mass of limestone that will cause a certain change in pH.

b i mass of limestone

ii pH after adding limestone

iii volume of water, pH before adding limestone

c i 20 g of limestone since the pond will then have a neutral pH, and this is the minimum mass that will cause this pH change.

ii The volume of water in the pond.

4 The Earth

4.1 The structure of the Earth

1 Top to bottom: crust, mantle, outer core, inner core

2A C, M, I

B O

C I

D M

E C

F C

3 Ships appear to sink over the horizon, the shadow of the Earth on the Moon is round, the Earth appears round when viewed from Space.

4a B and C

b A and D

4.2 Igneous rocks

1 magma, solidifies, igneous, gabbro, granite, basalt, non-porous, hard

2 There are no gaps between the crystals for water to soak into.

3a Sample 1 – the crystals are different colours.

b Sample 2 – its crystals are biggest

4 Basalt is used for road surfaces because it has a rough surface when it has not been polished. Granite is used for hotel floors because it is hard and durable. Gabbro is used for making sculptures because it can be polished to look attractive.

Extension

5 Gabbro is hard and durable.

4.3 Sedimentary rocks

1 Igneous: granite, basalt, gabbro, quartz
Sediment: limestone, sandstone, claystone, mudstone
Metamorphic: marble, slate, gneiss

2 transportation, deposition, compaction or cementation

3 (in any order)

a Sedimentary rocks are porous because they are made of grains with spaces between them.

b Sedimentary rocks are usually soft, this means that it is easy to scratch them.

c Igneous rocks are not porous because they are made of crystals with no space between them.

d Igneous rocks are usually hard, this means that, it is difficult to scratch them.

4a A

b B

c C – water soaked into the rock, but Marcello could not scratch it. The rock had both igneous and sedimentary properties.

Extension:

Physical: freeze thaw weathering. Water gets into cracks in rocks and freezes at night. Over time the cracks grow and the rock breaks.

Chemical: acidic rainwater. The acidic rainwater dissolves the rocks.

Biological: tree roots and lichens can damage rocks. Tree roots grow through cracks, making them larger and breaking the rock apart. Lichens make chemicals that break down rocks.

4.4 Sedimentary rock formation

1a B because it is made of grains with spaces between them.

b A because it is made of interlocking crystals.

2a D, bubbles came out of the rocks demonstrating that the rock was porous (because there are air spaces between the grains in the rock).

b C, igneous rock is non-porous as there are no gaps between the grains.

3 Sandstone – hard – building material
Claystone – easily moulded when wet – making bricks and pottery

4 A, D, B, E, C

5 Limestone is made from sediments, if creatures have been trapped in the sediment before decomposing and breaking down, a mineralised form of the sea creature can be formed.

Extension:

a Wind, water, gravity (through landslides).

b Deposition is when sediments stop moving and settle in layers

c In cementation, new minerals stick the sediments together whilst in compaction, the weight of the layers above squash the sediments together.

4.5 Metamorphic rocks

1 Marble, slate, and gneiss.

2a F – All sedimentary and igneous rocks can be changed into metamorphic rocks.

b F – Heat or high pressure (usually both) are needed to change an igneous or sedimentary rock to a metamorphic rock.

c T

d F – The rock does not get hot enough to melt.

e F – Technically, only heat or pressure are required but it is usually both.

f T

3 A – it is stripy.

4 Top to bottom:
Limestone: water will be absorbed, limestone is a sedimentary rock with gaps between the grains, allowing water to soak in.
Marble: water will not be absorbed, marble is made of tightly interlocking crystals with no gaps for the water.
Mudstone: water will be absorbed, mudstone is a sedimentary rock with gaps between the grains, allowing water to soak in.
Slate: water will not be absorbed, slate is made of tightly interlocking crystals with no gaps for the water.

Extension:

The left hand fossil. As slate is a metamorphic rock, any fossils within the rock would have been distorted/squashed when the rock was transformed.

4.6 Questions, evidence, and explanations

1

What Jack does	Stage of developing an explanation
Writes down that: The size of salol crystals may depend on the temperature of the surface the liquid salol cools on.	Suggest an explanation
Places liquid salol on warm and cold pieces of glass, and observes the crystals that form.	Ask a question
Looks carefully at his crystals and thinks about whether what he wrote down was correct.	Test the explanation
Wonders what causes salol to form crystals of different sizes.	Check the evidence

2

Statement	Evidence	Explanation
If you look at a cliff face made up of sedimentary rocks, you may see different layers of rock.	✔	
There are no spaces between the crystals of an igneous rock.	✔	
Sedimentary rocks were formed when sediments were deposited. In different time periods, different types of sediment were deposited.		✔
Water does not soak into igneous rocks.	✔	
Fossils found in slate have distorted shapes.	✔	
Igneous rocks do not contain fossils.	✔	
Slate was formed when high pressures squashed mudstone.		✔
Igneous rocks are formed from liquid rock. The liquid rock is hot, and living things cannot survive in it.		✔

Extension:

Ask a question: How is uplift involved in the formation of mountains?

Suggest an explanation: mountains are made of rocks that have been forced upwards by uplift.

Test the explanation: make observations of the rocks that mountains are made from, and similar kinds of rocks. Make a model of uplift.

Check the evidence: look carefully to see if the evidence shows that mountains could have been formed by uplift.

4.7 Using science to Explain predictions: volcanoes

1

Prediction	Scientific explanation
When the steepness of a volcano slope changes, the volcano may erupt.	This change may be caused by magma moving inside the volcano.
When there are more earth movements near a volcano, the volcano may erupt.	This change may be caused by magma moving upwards.
Magma often contains dissolved sulfur dioxide. When extra sulfur dioxide gas comes out of a volcano, the volcano may erupt.	This change may be caused by magma pushing up against surface rock.
When the surface temperature of a volcano changes, the volcano may erupt.	

2 Amisha: when rock cools quickly (e.g. when it comes into contact with water), the crystals form faster and are smaller.

Hakim: when rock cools slowly (e.g. underground near other heat sources), the crystals form slowly and are larger.

Gabir: rocks that are made up of separate grains have air spaces between the grains, allowing water to soak in.

3a Lisimba

b Muna

c Kibibi

4.8 Soil

1 Rock fragments – helps to give the soil its structure. Humus – a store of nutrients for microorganisms. Air – plants need this for respiration. Water – helps to give the soil its structure.

2a Humus

b 25%

c 10%

3a B

b D

c B

d D

Extension:

Add sand to the soil, since sand drains better than clay.

4.9 More about soil

1 pores, solid, less, more, loam

2 A, C, E, D, B

3a Hannah: 14 cm³

Ruth: 36 cm³

Rachel: 10 cm³

b Ruth's

4a maize, spinach

b Maiba's and Chenzira's

c Acid to lower the pH between 6.0 and 7.0.

4.10 Fossils

1a Mikayla

b Jayden: No mention of preservation.

Kaden: Does not state what fossils are but only how they are preserved.

Leah: Fossils can be remains or traces of animals or plants.

2a A – 1; B – 4; C – 6; D – 2; E – 3; F – 5.

b A, D, E, B, F, C

Extension:

Fossils are very rare as most dead animals or plants are eaten or decomposed. The conditions for fossilisation are very specific.

4.11 Estimating the age of the Earth

1a E

b A

c D

d C or E

2a F – Each time period has its own index fossil, the same fossil can be found in different rock types from the same time period.

b F – Index fossils are only some of the organisms that lived in that time period. There would have been other organisms however they might not have been fossilised.

c T

d T

3 B – P; C – Q; D – R.

4.12 Human fossils

1a Lucy was quickly buried in ash from a volcano.

b Lucy has a smaller bone ratio than modern chimpanzees, but a larger bone ratio than modern humans suggesting that Lucy may have walked on two legs. Lucy's skull volume is smaller than the modern human but larger than the modern chimpanzee.

c Lucy has a smaller skull volume than modern humans but a larger skull volume than that of the modern chimpanzee. This suggests that Lucy was an organism that had evolved from chimpanzees and was an ancestor of modern humans.

5   States of matter

5.1   The states of matter revisited

1 Lamorna and Fiona

2 water, flour, close together, air, far apart

3a freezing

b See image of a gas on p80 of the Student book.

c The particles gain energy and move around more.

d The nitrogen melts and changes to the liquid state – it would be able to flow and would take the shape of its container.

5.2   Explaining diffusion

1 A, C, B

2 move away from, randomly, mix with, evenly, continue to move

Extension:

a Ammonia particles will diffuse more quickly than hydrogen chloride particles because ammonia particles have a smaller mass.

b i Yes

ii More confident, since the evidence supports the explanation.

5.3   Explaining density

1a platinum

b mass = density × volume

mass = 7.86 × 4 = 31.44 g

2 C – the particles are less closely packed in liquid mercury than in solid mercury.

3 Balsa wood: 16/8 = 2 g/cm³

Oak wood: 42/6 = 7 g/cm³

Copper: 17.8/2 = 8.9 g/cm³

Aluminium: 2.7/1 = 2.7 g/cm³

Natural rubber: 1.5/5 = 0.3 g/cm³

4a 3 cm × 1 cm × 2 cm = 6 cm³

b 1 cm × 1 cm × 5 cm = 5 cm³

Extension:

The water particles are less closely packed in ice than in liquid water thus ice is less dense and can float on liquid water.

5.4   Explaining gas pressure

1a F – In a football, air particles are moving in all directions.

b T

c F – Air particles inside the football collide with the plastic and also with each other.

d F – At higher temperatures air particles move more quickly.

e F – The force exerted by air particles colliding with plastic pushes the plastic outwards.

f T

g T

2 In order: D, B, A, C, E

Extension:

Air pressure at the top of a mountain is lower than at sea level because there are fewer particles in the air at the top of a mountain. This means there are fewer collisions between air particles and a surface.

5.5   Ideas and evidence

1a S

b

c S

d S

e S

f

g S

h

2a top to bottom: iii, iv, i, ii

b iii and iv

c i

d i

e i and ii

f iv and i

3 Anything that could be investigated scientifically.

5.6 Doing an investigation

1a

Variable	change, measure or control?
temperature of liquid	change
diameter of tube	
height of liquid in tube	measure
mass of liquid	control

(temperature of liquid → change; diameter of tube → measure; height of liquid in tube → measure; mass of liquid → control)

i Esa

ii Esa and Hataki

b

Temperature of liquid (°C)	Height of liquid in tube (cm)

c X axis (horizontal): Temperature of liquid (°C)
Y axis (vertical): Height of liquid in tube (cm)

Extension:

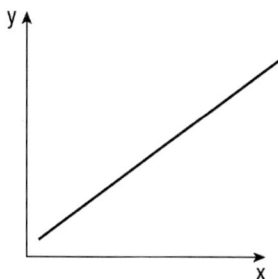

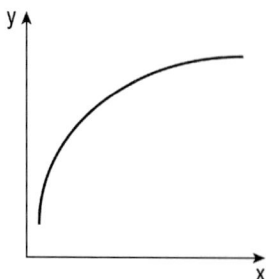

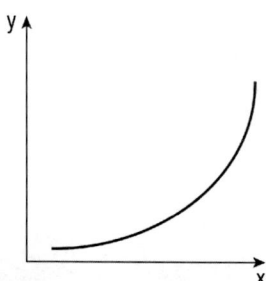

6 Material properties

6.1 Atoms

1a T

b F – An element cannot be broken into anything simpler.

c F – Some things are made of one type of element.

d T

e T

f F – There are 92 atoms that occur naturally on Earth.

g F – Scientists have made at least 25 elements.

h F – Atoms of platinum and silver are different.

2a B, C, D, F

b A and B, A and F, C and D

c B and F

d A and E

e C and D, A and B, A and F.

3 10,000,000,000,000

6.2 Elements and their symbols

1

Name of element	Symbol
hydrogen	H
helium	He
lithium	Li
beryllium	Be
boron	B
carbon	C
nitrogen	N
oxygen	O
fluorine	F
neon	Ne

2

Symbol	Name of element
Na	sodium
Mg	magnesium
Al	aluminium
Si	silicon
P	phosphorus
S	sulfur
Cl	chlorine
Ar	argon
K	potassium
Ca	calcium

3 sodium, strontium, scandium, silicon, selenium, sulfur, scandium, seaborgium, samarium, silver

4 calcium, carbon, chlorine, caesium, cobalt, chromium, copper, cadmium, cerium, californium

5 Revision is necessary

Extension:

a P

b Cl

c Be

6.3 Discovering the elements

1a i copper, silver, gold, iron, tin, lead
   ii These elements naturally exist on their own.
 b i hydrogen, nitrogen, oxygen, chlorine
   ii These elements are found in the air.
2a No other element had the same properties as the new element.
 b Information was not easily communicated internationally in the 1800s.
 c The strength of the cast iron samples were inconsistent.

6.4 Organising the elements

1a empirical
 b experiments
 c predictions
 d Mendeleev
 e mistakes
 f confident
 g Dalton
 h thinking
 i different
 j observations
 k evidence

Extension:
 a to determine whether or not he was correct
 b other scientists may have become more confident in Mendeleev's predictions are more accepting of them.

6.5 Interpreting data from secondary sources

1a It is easier to make a general comparison using a bar chart.
 b It is difficult to read the exact values from a bar chart.
 c The data is discrete.
 d As you move down group 2, the radius of the atom increases.
2a As you move down the group, the density increases.
 b In both tables, as you move down the group the density increases. The density increases in table A faster than in table B (8.9 to 22.5 for table A, 8.9 to 21.4 in table B).

3

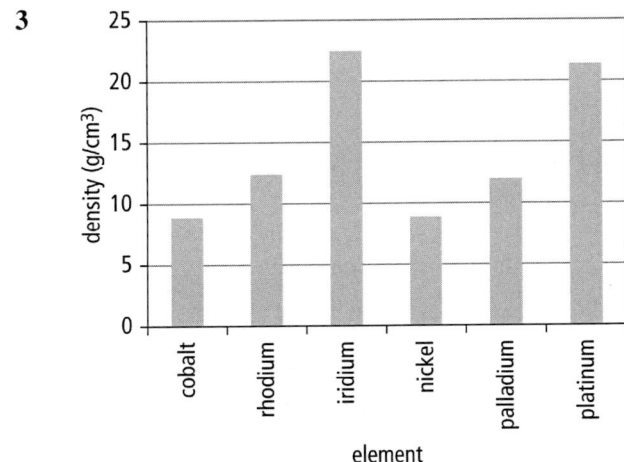

6.6 Explaining differences between metals and non-metals

1 Area right of the stepped line (B, Si etc). See the periodic table on p104 of the Student book.

2

Property	Typical metal	Typical non-metal
Conduction of heat	Good	Poor
Conduction of electricity	Good	Poor
Appearance	Shiny	Dull
Melting point and boiling point	High	Low

3a The atoms are close together so there are strong forces holding the atoms together. The metal has a high boiling point because much energy is required to overcome the forces holding the atoms together.
 b The metal is bendy because the layers can slide over each other.
4a There are weak forces holding the iodine molecules together. Iodine has a low melting point because less energy is required to overcome the forces holding the iodine molecules together.
 b There are weak forces holding the iodine molecules together, making them easy to break.

Extension:
A, C, D. Metals are good conductors of heat so have high thermal conductivity values.

6.7 What are compounds?

1 two, elements, are not, new

2

Substance	Element or compound?	State at 20 °C	One property or use of the substance
sodium	element	solid	Shiny metal
chlorine	element	gas	Green, smelly gas
sodium chloride	compound	solid	Used as food flavouring and preservative

3a carbon, oxygen
 b carbon, oxygen
 c sodium, iodine
 d iron, sulfur
 e hydrogen, oxygen
4a A, C, F
 b i B or D
   ii G
   iii A
   iv F
   v C
   vi B or D
   vii E or G

6.8 Making a compound

1a If the mass increases.

b **i** 30.74 – 30.50 = 0.24 g

ii 30.90 – 30.50 = 0.40 g

iii Yes, there is an increase in mass.

iv When I heated the magnesium, oxygen atoms from the air joined the magnesium atoms forming magnesium oxide. The mass of the product was greater (0.40 g) than the mass of the magnesium at the start (0.24 g) demonstrating that oxygen must have joined the magnesium.

c Anton may have made a mistake when measuring the mass the crucible and its contents.

6.9 Naming compounds and writing formulae

1a magnesium oxide

b iron sulfide

c aluminium chloride

d iron bromide

2a calcium, carbon, oxygen

b iron, sulfur, oxygen

c sodium, nitrogen, oxygen

3 top to bottom: carbon dioxide, 1 atom of carbon and 1 atom of oxygen, nitrogen dioxide, 1 atom of sulfur and 3 atoms of oxygen

4 iodine – I_2

dinitrogen tetroxide – N_2O_4

carbon monoxide – CO

carbon dioxide – CO_2

sulfur trioxide – SO_3

5 top to bottom:

KI

Li_2O

$NaNO_3$

$CaSO_4$

$MgCO_3$

6.10 Oxides, hydroxides, sulfates, and carbonates

1 compounds, oxygen, calcium, oxygen, acidic, carbon dioxide, less than, acids, bases, alkaline

2a sodium, hydrogen, oxygen

b potassium, hydrogen, oxygen

c zinc, sulfur, oxygen

d lithium, carbon, oxygen

3a magnesium oxide

b sodium hydroxide

c calcium carbonate

d copper sulfate

e nitrogen dioxide

f copper carbonate

4 top to bottom: K_2O, RbOH, $NiSO_4$, K_2CO_3

6.11 Chlorides

1 BA chloride is a compound of chlorine and one other element.

2a 125.8 g – 120.0 g = 5.8 g

b A, E, C, B, D, F

Extension:

Mapiro may have started off with less salt. Moyo may have ground the rock salt better. Moyo may have used more water, allowing more salt to dissolve. Any reasonable answer is acceptable.

6.12 Mixtures

1

	Mixtures of elements	Compounds
Can it easily be separated into its elements?	Yes	No
How do its properties compare to those of its elements?	Same	Different
Are its elements joined together?	No	Yes
Can you change the amounts of each elements in 100 g of the mixture or element?	Yes	No

2a M

b C

c M

d C

e M

f C

g M

3a B

b C

c A

d D

e E

4 A mixture of elements and compounds.

6.13 Separating mixtures – filtering and decanting

1a D

b N

c F

d N

e F

f D

2a salt water

b impurities

c **i** C

ii D

iii 80 g

6.14 Separating mixtures – evaporation and distillation

1 evaporation, salt, copper sulfate, solvent, solute, distillation, solute, pure water

2 Clockwise from top left: G, I, C, H & J, D, E, A, K & B, F

3 Anything plausible. Ideas need to include distillation of some fashion.

6.15 Separating mixtures – fractional distillation

1a Clockwise from top right: E, F, B, A, C, D
  b **i** ethanol
     ii 78 °C
2 The place where a mixture of vapours enters the column – C
   The hottest part of the column – B
   The coolest part of the column – A

Extension:
C, F, E, D, B, A

6.16 Separating mixtures – chromatography

1 B, D, F, A, C, E
2 Pen B
3 to determine the nutrients in a food
   test alcohol content in blood
   test for explosives.
4 Chromatogram, three, blue, most, least

6.17 Separating metals from their ores

1 Gold is more dense than sand. If carefully washed with water, the sand will wash away, leaving the gold behind.
2a From top to bottom:
   froth flotation
   copper iron sulfide floats
   waste materials
   heat with oxygen
  b copper sulfide + oxygen → copper + sulfur dioxide
3 $1000 \times (0.6/100) = 6$ g

6.18 What are you made of?

1 oxygen, hydrogen, nitrogen, carbon
2a water
  b hydrogen and oxygen
3a keratin
  b carbon, hydrogen, oxygen, nitrogen
4a 2.3 g
  b meat, beans, lentils, and dark green vegetables
  c Iron is a main component of haemoglobin which is used to transport oxygen round the body.
  d Tiredness, dizziness, weakness.

Extension:
Minerals to include:
Iron: tiredness, lack of energy, weakness.
Calcium: weak bones and frequent fractures.
Zinc: reduced growth in children, problems with senses and memory.
Iodine: swelling of thyroid gland, tiredness, brain damage.

7 Material changes

7.1 Chemical reactions

1A C   **C** C   **E** C   **G** R   **I** C
 B C   **D** B   **F** R   **H** R   **J** C
2

Change	Tick if change is a chemical reaction	Tick if change is reversible	Evidence
Boiling water		✔	The steam can be condensed into water.
Cooking potatoes	✔		The heat causes irreversible chemical changes within the potato – the potato can never be raw again.
Dissolving sugar in tea		✔	The sugar can separated from the tea using evaporation
A mango ripening	✔		There are irreversible chemical reactions within the mango which make it taste sweet. It is impossible to reverse these changes to make the mango unripe again
Lighting a match	✔		Once struck, the match catches fire, produces heat, light and different products which are characteristics of chemical reactions.

3a reactants: magnesium and oxygen, products: magnesium oxide

b reactants: carbon and oxygen, products: carbon dioxide

Extension:

The product of magnesium and oxygen is solid magnesium oxide which remains. The product of carbon and oxygen is the gas carbon dioxide which escape the container into the surrounding air.

7.2 Writing word equations

1

word or symbol	meaning
reactant	Reacts to make.
product	The chemicals you make in a chemical reaction.
→	The chemical you start with in a chemical reaction.

2a reactants: magnesium and oxygen, products: magnesium oxide

b reactants: iron and oxygen, products: iron oxide

c reactants: carbon and oxygen, products: carbon dioxide

d reactants: sodium hydroxide and hydrochloric acid, products: sodium chloride and water

e reactants: hydrochloric acid and copper oxide, products: copper chloride and water

3a zinc oxide

b oxygen

c oxygen

d sulfur

4a lithium + oxygen → lithium oxide

b calcium + oxygen → calcium oxide

c zinc + oxygen → zinc oxide

5a water

b copper sulfide

6a calcium carbonate + calcium oxide → carbon dioxide

b aluminium + iodine → aluminium iodide

c magnesium + sulfuric acid → magnesium sulfate + hydrogen

d copper oxide + magnesium → magnesium oxide + copper

7.3 Corrosion reactions

1 on the surface, destroy, slowly, oxygen, rust, exposes, can

2 iron + oxygen + water → hydrated iron oxide

3a copper carbonate

b silver sulfide

4

Method of preventing corrosion	Stops air and water being in contact with the iron	Reacts with oxygen and / or water instead of the iron
Covering with grease	✔	
Attaching a piece of zinc to the iron		✔
Painting	✔	
Covering the iron in a thin layer of tin	✔	

Extension:

a The iron reacted with water and oxygen in the water, forming hydrated iron oxide (rust).

b In theory, by removing water from the air the iron cannot react with water and oxygen to form rust.

7.4 Doing an investigation

1a

Variable	change	measure or observe	control
Volume of solution			✔
Mass of salt dissolved in water	✔		
Temperature of solution			✔
The metal the nail is made out of			✔
Amount of rust made after 1 week		✔	
Size of nail			✔

b mass of salt dissolved in water (g)

c The variable he changes is continuous and the variable he observes is continuous.

d The 'amount of rust made after 1 week' is an inacurate measurement dependent on the observer.

7.5 Using reactions to identify chemicals

1a lithium: crimson

sodium: yellow

potassium: lilac

calcium: red

barium: green

2 iron(II) chloride: green
iron(III) chloride: brown
copper sulfate: blue

3a copper hydroxide

b iron(II) hydroxide

c iron(III) hydroxide

4 (precipitate is underlined)

a copper sulfate + sodium hydroxide →
<u>copper hydroxide</u> + sodium sulfate

b iron(II) chloride + sodium hydroxide →
<u>iron(II) hydroxide</u> + sodium chloride

c copper chloride + sodium hydroxide →
<u>copper hydroxide</u> + sodium chloride

d iron(III) nitrate + potassium hydroxide →
<u>iron(III) hydroxide</u> + potassium nitrate

5 lithium

6 copper

8 Material properties

8.1 Atomic structure

1

Phenomenon	The solid sphere model of atoms *can* explain this.	The solid sphere model of atoms *cannot* explain this.
Diffusion	✔	
Chemical reactions		✔
Changes of state	✔	
Atoms joining together		✔

2

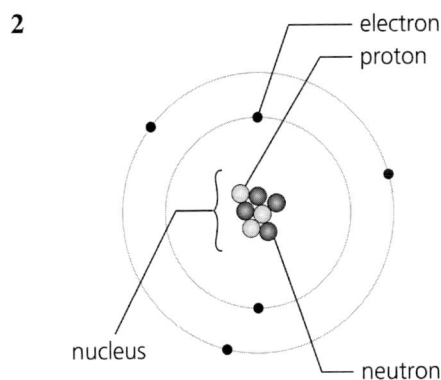

electron
proton
nucleus
neutron

3

Sub-atomic particle	Relative charge	Relative mass
Proton	+1	1
Neutron	0	1
Electron	−1	$\frac{1}{1840}$

4a 5

b 19

c 28

d 33

5a

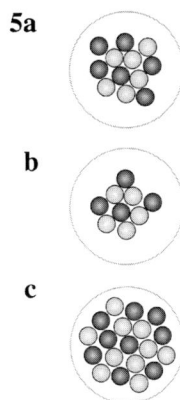

b

c

Extension:

In an atom of beryllium, there are 4 protons, 4 electrons and 5 neutrons with a total relative mass of 9 and 5/1840. The majority of the mass (99.97% of the atom's mass) is in the centre of the atom whilst the remaining is found in the outside of the atom.

8.2 Finding electrons

1a From top to bottom: i, iii, ii, iv

b The cathode ray bent towards the positively-charged metal suggesting that the cathode ray is negatively-charged (because it is made up of electrons).

c think creatively

Extension:

A paragraph comparing the findings from the table.

8.3 Discovering the nucleus

1a A or B or C or F

b D or E

c G

2 nucleus, mass, positive, electrons, orbitals

3

Observation	Explanation
Most particles travel straight through the foil.	These particles travelled very close to a positively-charged nucleus.
A very few particles bounce backwards off the foil.	These particles hit a positively-charged nucleus.
Some particles change direction slightly when they travel through the foil.	These particles travelled through the empty space between nuclei.

(Note: observations and explanations are cross-matched as shown by the crossing lines.)

Extension:

4a explanation

b evidence

c prediction

8.4 Protons, electrons, and the periodic table

1a F – The nucleus is made of protons and neutrons.

b T

c F – The first electron shell can hold two electrons.

d F – The number of protons is equal to the number of electrons.

2

Element	Number of electrons in an atom of the element	Electronic structure
helium	2	**2**
lithium	**3**	2, 1
boron	5	**2, 3**
nitrogen	7	**2, 5**
fluorine	9	**2, 8, 1**
magnesium	**10**	2, 8, 2
silicon	14	**2, 8, 4**
sulfur	16	**2.8.6**

3   See diagrams on page 153 of the Student book.

Extension:

Electronic structures of group 1 elements	Electronic structures of group 2 elements
Lithium: 2,1 Sodium: 2,8,1 Potassium: 2,8,8,1	Beryllium: 2,2 Magnesium: 2,8,2 Calcium: 2,8,8,2

As you move down the group, the number of shells increases, but the number of electrons in the outer shell remains the same/is the same as the group number.

8.5   Proton number, nucleon number, and isotopes

1

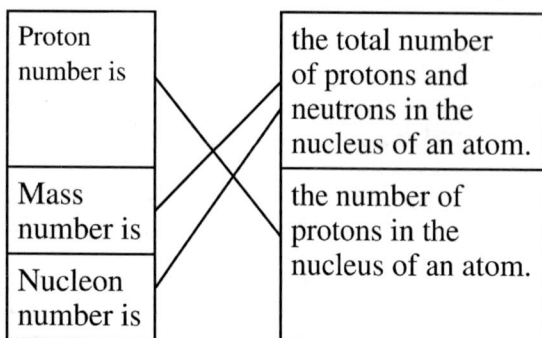

Proton number is	the total number of protons and neutrons in the nucleus of an atom.
Mass number is	the number of protons in the nucleus of an atom.
Nucleon number is	

2

75	23	53	14	8	7	53	16	9	92	7
Re	V	I	Si	O	N	I	S	F	U	N

Revision is fun.

3

Atom of the element…	Proton number	Nucleon number	Number of neutrons
Hydrogen	1	1	**0**
Helium	2	**4**	2
Beryllium	4	9	**5**
Nitrogen	7	**14**	7
Sodium	11	23	**12**
Sulfur	16	**32**	16
Titanium	22	**48**	26

4a   3
b   4
c   silicon
d   gallium
e   half
f   neon

8.6   The Group 1 elements

1a   A, O
b   A, O
c   O
d   O
e   O
f   O
2a   i   lithium + water → lithium **hydroxide** + hydrogen
ii   sodium + **water** → **sodium hydroxide** + hydrogen
iii   potassium + **water** → **potassium hydroxide** + **hydrogen**
b   As you move down the group, the reactions of Group 1 metals with water becom more vigorous.
3a   Top to bottom: 0.53 g/cm³, 21.43 g/cm³, 0.86 g/cm³, 20 g/cm³.
b   A, C, both of these metals have low densities.

Extension:

a

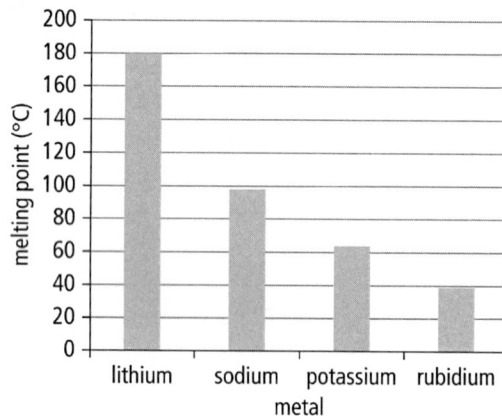

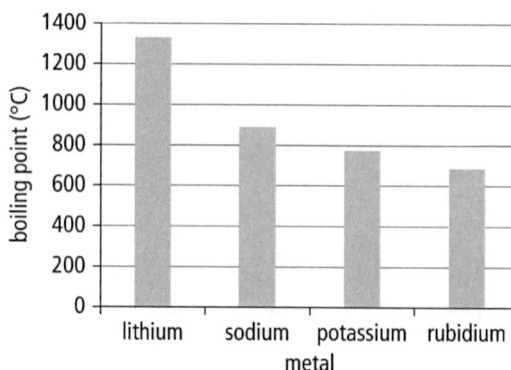

b   The melting and boiling points decrease as you move down the group.

8.7   The Group 2 elements

1   Second group (column) on the periodic table shaded in.
2a   Bubbles more vigorously (more than calcium but less than barium). Colourless solution formed.

b calcium + water → calcium hydroxide + hydrogen

c barium + water → barium hydroxide + hydrogen

3a calcium chloride + water + hydrogen

b calcium + hydrochloric acid → calcium chloride + water + hydrogen

Extension:

a

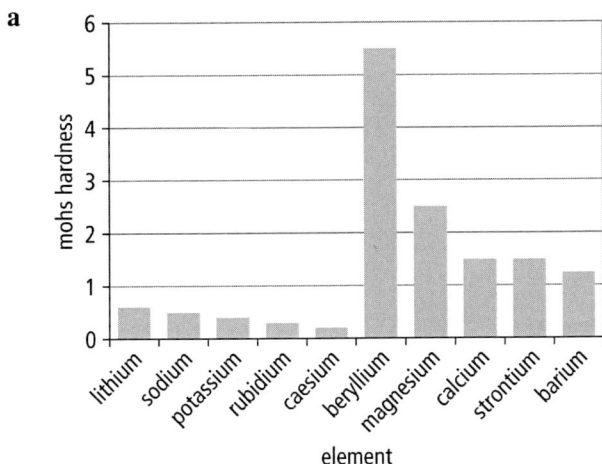

b The hardness values for Group 2 decrease as you move down the group.

c Both Group 1 and Group 2 elements decrease in hardness as you move down the group. The group 2 elements are almost 10 times harder than group 1. In both groups, the reactions with water become more vigorous as you move down the group.

8.8 The group 7 elements

1a chlorine

b iron bromide

c iodine

d potassium bromide

e chlorine

f sodium chloride

2 There are strong forces between the two atoms of a chlorine molecule.

There are weak forces between a chlorine molecule and its neighbours.

There are strong forces between the two atoms of a iodine molecule.

There are weak forces between a iodine molecule and its neighbours.

4a 7

b 7

c B

d 7

e B

f 7

g 1

h B

Extension:

Most: potassium and fluorine,

Least: lithium and iodine

8.9 Looking at secondary data

1 Larger sample numbers makes the results more reliable and reduces errors.

2 To compare the affect of fluoridation with no fluoridation.

3 2007–2012 is a larger time frame so she would be able to determine the affects of fluoridation over a longer time period.

4 In towns where the water was fluoridated, the number of 5–6 year olds with missing teeth (from tooth disease) and the number of 12–13 year olds with surface decay decreased however the same affect was seen in town D which did not have access to chlorinated water.

5 If the water did not contain adequate levels of fluorine, it is possible that the affects of the fluorine may have not been as significant as if the correct levels of fluorine were used.

8.10 Periodic trends

1a 7th group (penultimate column)

b 2nd row (Li, Be, B, C, N, O, F, Ne)

c 4th row (K, Ca, Sc, Ti, V,Cr, Mn, Fe, Co, Ni, Cu, Zn, Ga, Ge, As, Se, Br, Kr)

2a It is not possible to measure the covalent radius of an atom in a school laboratory (no suitable equipment).

b **i** A bar chart. The data is discrete.

ii

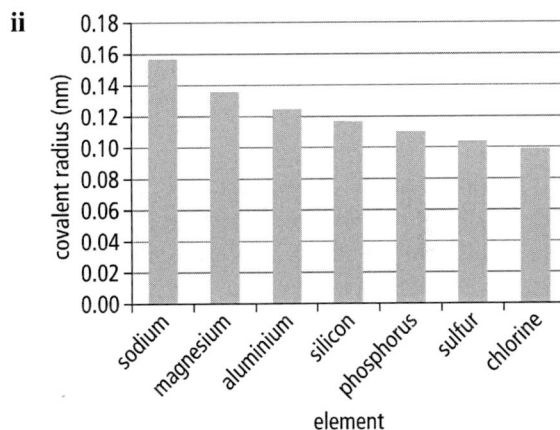

c As you move across the period, the covalent radius decreases.

Extension:

The radius of atoms decreases as you move across (left to right) period 3 of the periodic table. The rate at which the elements decrease in size decreases as you move across the period. Chitra needed to specify which group and/or use some form of data.

8.11 How scientists work: inside sub-atomic particles

1a

Statement describing what scientists did	Stage of developing a scientific explanation
Scientists suggested that there is a particle called the Higgs boson that gives protons and neutrons their mass. They described the properties of this particle.	**A** Use creative thought to suggest an explanation.
Scientists built the Large Hadron Collider. They made protons collide in it. They examined the products of the collisions.	**B** Check the evidence to see if it supports the suggested explanation.
Scientists wondered what gives protons and neutrons their mass.	**C** Ask a question.
Scientists compared the products of the collisions with the predicted properties of the Higgs boson.	**D** Collect evidence to test the suggested explanation.

b C, A, D, B

c There would be a larger number of people who would look at it. The best physicists in lots of different countries could work with the data.

d To be certain that they have and to continue any other research.

2a International communications Modern technology makes it possible for people to communicate quickly over long distances.

b Top to bottom: B, A, A, D.

9 Energy changes

9.1 Energy changes in chemical reactions

1 Exothermic changes release heat to the surroundings.
Exothermic changes include combustion reactions.
Endothermic changes include evaporation.
Endothermic reactions take in heat from the surroundings.
Endothermic changes include melting.

2 melt, cold, takes in, start, endothermic

3a B: +48
D: −13
E: +61

b A, B, E

c E

d C, D

e C, D

f A, B, E

Extension:
Energy is taken in from the surroundings, giving the particles enough energy to overcome the forces holding the particles together as a liquid.

9.2 Investigating fuels

1a top to bottom: control, change, control, measure

b To find out if his experiment will work.

c **i** to reduce error, to make the results more reliable

ii butanol (81)

iii 40

iv Butanol releases the most energy when it burns, methanol releases the least.

Extension:
Some of the heat released would have heated up the surrounding area.

9.3 Choosing fuels

1a

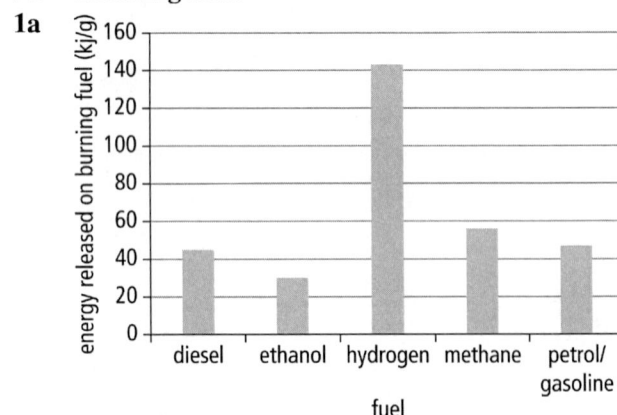

b ethanol, diesel, petrol/gasoline, methane, hydrogen

c Diesel, ethanol and petrol are liquids at room temperature.

d hydrogen

e **i** Ethanol: made from crops (which are grown).

   ii Hydrogen: made from methane (which can be produced easily from natural resources).

   iii Methane: made from animal waste and rubbish (which is renewable).

f Sensible comparisons using facts from the table.

9.4 Calculating food energy

1a Top to bottom: wear gloves and be careful when moving around.
Ensure that anyone with allergies is not in the room.

b 100 cm^3, this volume provides a reasonable temperature change without boiling the water.

c **i** To reduce errors and make the results more reliable.

   ii

Nut	Temperature change 1 (°C)	Temperature change 2 (°C)	Temperature change 3 (°C)	Average temperature change (°C)
1				
2				
3				

d **i** cashew nut, peanut, walnut

   ii There is a difference of 6 °C between the highest and lowest values. There could have been some anomalies. Cerena didn't state the mass of the nuts she would use.

9.5 Investigating endothermic changes

1 takes in, from, freezes, cools down

2a **i** top to bottom: control, change, control, measure, control

   ii Keeping these variables the same makes the results comparable/fair test.

b top to bottom: −13, −6, +23, +7

c Habibah is correct. Solutes A and B are the two endothermic reactions and solute A is the most endothermic.

10 The reactivity series

10.1 The reactions of metals with oxygen

1 oxygen, oxides, iron oxide, element, compound

2a lithium, potassium, sodium

b gold, platinum

c potassium, sodium, lithium, platinum/gold

3a oxygen

b iron oxide

c potassium

d lead oxide

e oxygen

f zinc

Extension:

order of reactivity (most to least reactive): magnesium, zinc, copper, iron.

10.2 The reactions of metals with water

1a

Hazard symbol	Meaning of hazard symbol	Action to reduce risk from hazard
	corrosive	Wear eye protection.
		Use a tiny piece of potassium.
		Place a screen between the glass trough and the students.
	highly flammable	Do not touch the metal – handle with forceps.
		Replace the lid on the potassium container as soon as possible.
		Wear gloves.

b **i** It was easy for Mr Fissoo to cut the potassium.

   ii The potassium floated.

   iii The potassium moved around quickly.

   iv There was a red flame.

   v The Universal Indicator solution changed colour from green to blue.

2a T

b F – Calcium reacts with water to make calcium hydroxide and hydrogen gas.

c T

d F – sodium + water → sodium hydroxide + hydrogen

10.3 The reactions of metals with acids

1a copper and gold

b magnesium

c magnesium, zinc, iron, copper/gold

2a Place a lit splint into the gas. If the splint goes out and makes a squeaky pop, the gas is hydrogen.

b **i** hydrogen

   ii zinc sulfide

   iii hydrochloric acid, hydrogen

   iv zinc, hydrogen

Extension:

a magnesium, water, magnesium chloride

b Filter out the magnesium, evaporate the water off to leave magnesium chloride.

10.4 The reactivity series

1a potassium

b gold

c magnesium, calcium, lithium, sodium, potassium

d lead, copper, silver, gold

2a Use the same amounts of metal, use the same amount of hydrochloric acid.

b zinc

3a copper

b zinc + oxygen → zinc oxide

4

Metal	Observation
magnesium	no reaction
calcium	bubbles vigorously
copper	small bubbles on surface of metal

(magnesium → bubbles vigorously, calcium → small bubbles on surface of metal, copper → no reaction — lines crossed)

Extension:

Zinc and magnesium are more reactive than the iron so the zinc/magnesium corrode instead of the iron.

10.5 Tin in the reactivity series

1a **i** Tin is more reactive as it reacts with hydrochloric acid whilst copper does not.

ii To collect some preliminary data and to make sure the investigation would work.

b **i** zinc

ii tin

iii Tin is below zinc and above lead in the reactivity series.

c **i** Iron is between lead and zinc in the reactivity series. Senni can use this information to determine the location of tin in relation to iron.

ii Resources/ reliability of data.

iii Based on the data from **b** and **iii**, tin is less reactive than iron, making the reactivity series as follows: zinc, iron, tin, lead.

10.6 Metal displacement reactions

1 copper, iron sulfate, displacement, more, copper, displaces, more, less

2 See the table at the bottom of the page.

3a iron + copper sulfate solution → iron sulfate + copper

b magnesium + lead nitrate solution → magnesium nitrate + lead

c iron + copper oxide → iron oxide + copper

d zinc + iron nitrate solution → zinc nitrate + iron

e zinc + lead oxide → zinc oxide + lead

f magnesium + copper chloride solution → magnesium chloride + copper

Extension:

a aluminium and iron oxide

b Lots of sparks and molten iron.

c aluminium + iron oxide → aluminium oxide + iron

10.7 Extracting metals from their ores

1 more, more, more, more

2a aluminium, magnesium, calcium, lithium, sodium, and potassium are removed using electrolysis

b zinc, iron, lead, copper

c silver, gold

3 Carbon is more reactive than some metals so it can be used to displace the metals from their oxides. Some metals are more reactive than carbon so must be extracted using electrolysis.

4a tin + carbon dioxide

b lead + carbon dioxide

5 iron sulfate + copper

Extension:

a sodium and magnesium

b sodium + titanium chloride → titanium + sodium chloride

magnesium + titanium chloride → titanium + magnesium chloride

10.8 Writing symbol equations

1a O_2

b N_2O_2

c 2

d 8

e 2

2a S + O_2 → SO_2

b $2Zn$ + O_2 → $2ZnO$

c Mg + $2HCl$ → $MgCl_2$ + H_2

d Zn + H_2SO_4 → $ZnSO_4$ + H_2

e $2Na$ + $2H_2O$ → $2NaOH$ + H_2

f $2K$ + $2H_2O$ → $2KOH$ + H_2

g Mg + CuO → MgO + Cu

h $CuSO_4$ + Fe → Cu + $FeSO_4$

3a C + O_2 → CO_2

b $2Mg$ + O_2 → $2MgO$

c Zn + $2HCl$ → $ZnCl_2$ + H_2

d $2Li$ + $2H_2O$ → $2LiOH$ + H_2

e $TiCl_4$ + $2Mg$ → $2MgCl_2$ + Ti

compound / metal	magnesium chloride solution	iron chloride solution	lead nitrate solution	copper oxide
magnesium	(shaded)	✔	✔	✔
zinc		✔	✔	✔
iron		(shaded)	✔	✔
lead			(shaded)	✔
copper				(shaded)

11 Making salts

11.1 Making salts – acids and metals
1 Dasbala
2a chloride
 b nitric *nitrate*
 c sulfate
3 A, D, F, B, E, C
4a zinc chloride
 b magnesium sulfate
 c magnesium chloride
 d iron sulfate
5 Place a lit splint inside a container with the gas. If the splint goes out and a squeaky pop sound is made, the gas was hydrogen.

11.2 Making salts – acids and carbonates
1 See the table at the bottom of the page.
2a copper chloride
 b carbon dioxide
3a copper carbonate + hydrochloric acid → **copper chloride + carbon dioxide** + water
 b zinc carbonate + sulfuric acid → **zinc sulfate** + carbon dioxide + **water**
 c magnesium carbonate + **nitric acid** → magnesium nitrate + **carbon dioxide + water**
 d **copper carbonate** + sulfuric acid → copper sulfate + carbon dioxide + **water**
4a The carbonate will stop bubbling.
 b B, E, F
 c E, F

Extension:
The direct heating causes the copper sulfate to spit, losing some of the product as well as being a danger. Heating indirectly over a water bath ensures even evaporation and reduces the amount of product lost.

11.3 Making salts – acids and alkalis
1a Sodium chloride
 b Sodium nitrate
 c Potassium sulfate
 d Potassium chloride
2a hydrochloric acid + sodium hydroxide → **sodium chloride** + water
 b **nitric acid** + sodium hydroxide → sodium nitrate **+ water**
 c nitric acid + potassium hydroxide → **potassium nitrate + water**
 d hydrochloric acid + **potassium chloride** → potassium chloride + **water**

3a i Use a **measuring cylinder** to accurately measure 25.00 cm³ of sodium carbonate solution.
 ii Place this solution in a **conical flask**. Add a few drops of Universal indicator solution.
 iii Add hydrochloric acid to the sodium carbonate solution and indicator. Stop adding when the mixture is **green**.
 iv Add charcoal powder to the mixture. Filter the mixture. Keep the **colourless** solution.
 v Pour the solution into an **evaporating basin**.
 vi Heat the solution until **half the solution has evaporated. Place the evaporating basin in a warm place for several days for the remaining water to evaporate.**
 b So he can determine when the sodium carbonate has been neutralized.
 c To remove the charcoal powder (which has removed the colour).

11.4 Making salts – fertilisers
1a To increase the nutrient content in the soil and increase crop yields.
 b manure and compost
 c nitrogen, phosphorus, potassium
 d nitrogen, hydrogen
2a T
 b F – The reaction also produces water.
 c T
 d T
 e F – The volume of acid required is also dependent on the concentration of the ammonium nitrate.
 f F – To make ammonium sulfate, you need to react ammonium hydroxide with sulfuric acid.
3 From left to right: ammonia solution, burette, conical flask, litmus paper, glass rod, evaporating dish, pipette, nitric acid

12 Rates of reaction

12.1 Rates of reaction
1a Rusting
 b Reactions that make useful chemicals e.g. soap, fertilisers, medicines.
2a calcium carbonate + **hydrochloric acid** → **calcium chloride** + carbon dioxide + water
 b The gas made in the reaction is soluble in water.
 c i In this section the volume of gas is increasing quickly. **D**
 v The reaction is happening quickly. **E**

	copper carbonate	magnesium carbonate	zinc carbonate
hydrochloric acid	*copper chloride*	*magnesium chloride*	*zinc chloride*
nitric acid	*copper nitrate*	magnesium nitrate	*zinc nitrate*
sulfuric acid	*copper sulfate*	*magnesium sulfate*	*zinc sulfate*

Box 2
ii The reaction is slowing down. **E**
iv In this section the volume of gas is increasing slowly. **D**

Box 3
iii In this section the volume of gas is not changing. **D**
vi The reaction has finished. **E**

12.2 Concentration and reaction rate

1a i Flavia
ii Harry
iii Rebecca

b Top to bottom: change, control, control, measure, control, control

2 The diagram on the right, since there are more acid particles in the same volume of solution.

3 collide, more, collide, faster

Extension:

Diagrams similar to those in 12.2 (page 213) of Student book.
Labelled beaker and acid particles.

12.3 Temperature and reaction rate

1a i Ebba
ii Wanda

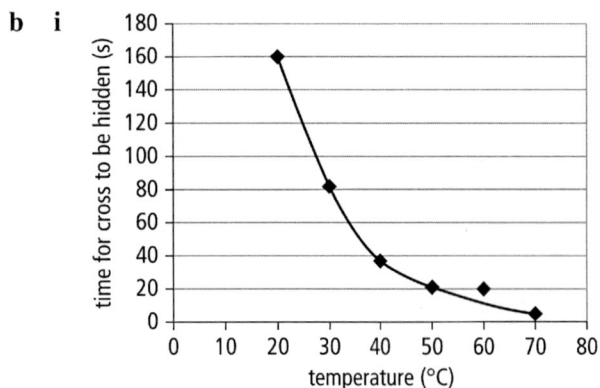

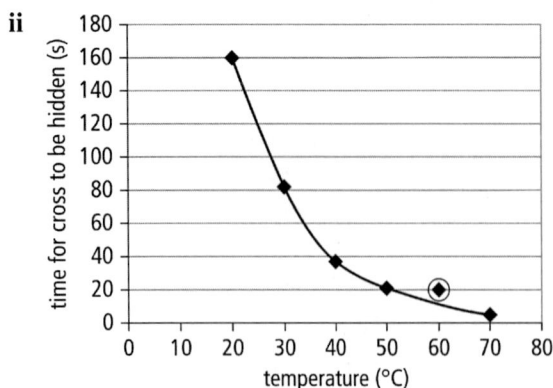

b i

y-axis: time for cross to be hidden (s); x-axis: temperature (°C)

ii

y-axis: time for cross to be hidden (s); x-axis: temperature (°C)

iii By repeating the investigation, the student can reduce error and make the investigation more reliable.
iv The variables are both continuous.

c At higher temperatures, the particles have more energy and collide more frequently. Therefore, the rate of reaction is faster.

12.4 Surface area and reaction rate

1 A

2a Carbon dioxide is a gas and escapes into the air.

b i

Size of pieces	Time for mass to decrease by 0.8 g
Big	140
Medium	93
Powder	30

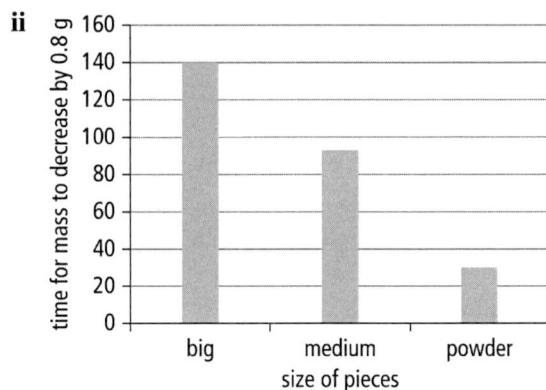

ii

y-axis: time for mass to decrease by 0.8 g; x-axis: size of pieces (big, medium, powder)

iii Increasing the surface area of the calcium carbonate increases the number of particles that can react with the hydrochloric acid, increasing the rate of reaction.

12.5 Catalysts and reaction rate

1 temperature, concentration, surface area, catalyst, is not, amylase, glucose.

2a hydrogen peroxide → water + oxygen
b Place a glowing splint into the gas. If the splint relights, the gas is oxygen.
i Manganese(IV) oxide
ii Iron oxide and zinc oxide

Extension:

a Catalysts speed up reactions without themselves being used up in the reaction.

b Platinum, rhodium, and palladium are used in catalytic converters to remove carbon monoxide from car fumes. Iron catalyses the production of ammonia from hydrogen and nitrogen when producing fertilisers.

1a i freezing

ii When a liquid freezes, its particles stop moving around from place to place. They arrange themselves in a regular pattern, and vibrate on the spot.

b See the diagram of particles in a gas at the top of page 80 of the Student book.

c i increases

ii When in the liquid state, all the particles are touching. In the gas state, none of the particles touch and they are spread out, thus the volume must increase to accommodate this.

d liquid, gas

2a Scented particles move randomly in the air, spreading out and mixing with the air particles. When these particles enter Hanan's nose, she can smell them.

b The particles have more energy. The particles move faster

3a There would be fewer air particles.

b i As the number of air particles increases, the pressure on the inside of the ball increases.

ii There are more air particles in the same volume so there are more collisions of air particles against the inside of the wall.

4a

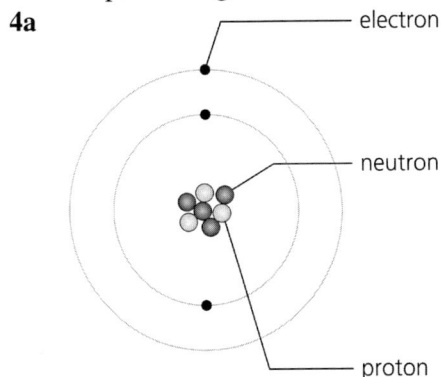

b Na, K

c i 2 electrons in the inner shell, 8 in the middle shell, 1 in the outer shell.

ii 2,8,1

iii All three elements have 1 electron in the outer shell.

d i flammable

ii corrosive

e i Sodium whizzes around on the surface of the water. Bubbles are produced quickly, the Universal Indicator changes from green to purple.

ii potassium hydroxide + hydrogen

iii The potassium hydroxide that is produced is alkaline. Universal Indicator turns purple in the presence of alkali.

5a B

b C

c D

6a Use a magnet to attract the iron, leaving the sulfur behind.

b i Sulfur

ii Iron sulfide is chemically bonded whilst iron and sulfur are not and can be easily separated. The properties of iron and sulfur are different from iron sulfide

7a i type of nail, volume of water

ii To ensure that they do not affect the results/ keep the investigation a fair test.

b i oxygen, water

ii The grease prevents oxygen and water from interacting with the nail.

iii The paint prevented the oxygen and water from interacting with the nail. The oxygen and water could interact with the nail where the paint was scratched which is why it rusted.

iv As magnesium is more reactive than iron, it can act as a 'sacrificial metal', reacting with the oxygen and water instead of the iron.

8a Igneous

b A type of rock formed when an igneous rock or a sedimentary rock was changed by heat, or pressure, or heat and pressure.

c i 3

ii F – this rock is a sedimentary rock that is found beneath two other sedimentary rocks. It is the lowest layer, so it must be older than the sedimentary rocks D and E.

iii A fossil is the remains or traces of a plant or animal that lived many years ago.

iv Rocks B and F contain the same fossil. Geologists use index fossils to date sedimentary rocks. Layers of rock that contain the same fossils are the same age.

9a A & C, B & C.

b Exothermic, the temperature of the solutions increased.

10a iron, copper, or gold

b i hydrogen

ii sodium and magnesium

c i B

ii copper + zinc sulfate

iii displacement

11 A, D, F, B, C, E, G

Cambridge International Examinations bears no responsibility for the example answers to questions taken from its past question papers which are contained in this publication.

1a A metal, B non-metal, C non-metal, D non-metal, E non-metal

b There is a change from metal to non-metal.

c **i** See the structure of sodium on page 153 of the Student book.

ii $Na \rightarrow Na^+ + e^-$

d The missing words in order are: soft, increase, lithium, basic.

2a calcium, magnesium, iron, copper

b bubbles produced steadily with no spitting

c **i** It floats on top of the magnesium chloride.

ii Magnesium is more reactive than carbon.

iii To prevent magnesium reacting with oxygen.

iv Any noble gas or nitrogen.

d **i** carbon monoxide + water $\rightleftharpoons$ carbon dioxide + hydrogen

ii reversible reaction

iii Add aqueous sodium hydroxide or ammonia: a red-brown precipitate forms.

3a **i** A thermometer, B flask, C measuring cylinder

ii calcium carbonate + hydrochloric acid $\rightarrow$ calcium chloride + carbon dioxide + water

iii 80 s

iv The sketched slope should be steeper but flatten out at the same volume (80 cm^3).

v It slows down when concentration is decreased, but increases with temperature.

4a **i** The temperature of the water rises.

ii ethanol + oxygen $\rightarrow$ carbon dioxide + water

b coal, natural gas, wood, petrol, paraffin

c **i** painting, galvanising, covering with plastic, sacrificial protection

ii contains water molecules

iii high boiling point or melting point, high density, can act as catalyst; forms coloured compounds

5a limestone, marble or chalk

b **i** Crops grow best in soil with a pH close to 7.

ii Calcium carbonate will not be washed away easily by rain. Since it is insoluble it cannot make the soil's pH too high. Calcium oxide could be washed away, and if present in excess the pH of the soil could rise above 7. Also calcium oxide is more expensive since it is obtained by heating calcium carbonate.

iii Building houses.

6a **i** as heat

ii exothermic

iii $\rightarrow 2CO_2 + 3H_2O$

iv The students should mark the points on the vertical lines. Accept answers of between 2640 and 2700 kJ/mol for the heat of combustion.

v same general formula, same functional group which leads to similar chemical properties; chain length increases by one C at a time, leading to a trend in physical properties (e.g. an increase in boiling point)

7a C

b **i** $2Na + 2H_2O \rightarrow 2NaOH + H_2$

ii It floats on water / moves across surface / forms a ball / disappears.

iii blue, because the solution is alkaline (sodium hydroxide)

iv It reacts with chlorine to form sodium chloride, and it reacts readily with oxygen.

c The reaction is faster.

d **i** atoms of the same element, with different numbers of neutrons

ii 11

iii 19

8a The six missing numbers for W, in order down the column, are: 0, 15, 32, 36, 37, 37. The six missing numbers for X, in order down the column, are: 0, 29, 34, 36, 37, 37.

b Students may find it easier to draw the curves if they use a large scale on the x-axis. Time (the independent variable) should be marked on the x-axis, and volume on the y-axis. Curve X will be steeper, but both curves finish at the same volume.

c X: the steeper slope on the graph shows a faster reaction.

d The final volume of oxygen is the same in both experiments because the same amount of hydrogen peroxide was used in both experiments.

e The graph should have a steeper slope than X, but the final gas volume will be the same.

Notes

Notes

Notes

137